The Poems of PROPERTIUS

The Poems of
PROPERTIUS

translated by Constance Carrier
with introduction, notes, and glossary
by Palmer Bovie

Indiana University Press
Bloomington

For Galen

CONTENTS

SEXTUS PROPERTIUS

Little is known of the life of Sextus Propertius. He was a Roman citizen, and an Italian who like St. Francis and Raphael came from the region of Umbria. He was born, probably at Assisi, around 50 B.C., and died some forty years later after earning recognition as a lyric poet whose main theme was love. Propertius' father died while Propertius was still a boy, and his mother during Propertius' early manhood; so the poet seems to have grown up and followed his literary inclinations alone and unguided. The loss of his patrimony in the confiscations of 41-40 B.C. meant reduced circumstances, and Propertius turned away from the public career for which his conventional rhetorical education had prepared him, to become a poet instead. His morality, like a painter's, consisted in "getting up before noon and keeping his brushes dry." His attention, like a mystic's, was concentrated on the most important person he could name, Cynthia.

Love for this mistress, which took the form of an ungovernable passion, "taught me," Propertius says, "to hate chaste young women and abandon any thought of a career." But he enjoyed a career, nevertheless, to which his 92 elegies bear various and ample witness. Because of these poems, distributed in four successive books, he came to rank alongside Catullus and Ovid and to be thought of as something like the brother-poet of his slightly older contemporary, Tibullus. Ovid himself listed Propertius in the conventional canon of writers of love lyrics; Horace paid him a left-handed compliment in *The Epistle to Florus;* Quintilian pointed out that some critics rated Propertius first among elegiac poets, although he himself would place Tibullus first and Propertius second on the list.

Tibullus and Propertius both wrote love poetry in the same form, the elegiac meter (one hexameter line alternating with one slightly shorter pentameter line), often in the same vein and often similar in subject and decorative detail. Each had a mistress to whom significantly passionate poems are addressed, each mentions a minor woman but is preoccupied with contending for the favors of the main woman in his life and so becomes expert on the general subject of being in love. Tibullus is the quiet, clear and craftsmanlike poet; Propertius is the daring, difficult, experimental writer. Tibullus largely and Propertius occasionally evoke the pastoral imagery that regularly adorns the classical miming for being in love—a rural, enameled background as the chief scenery in which their lilting couplets pirouette to describe love as the dominant experience.

But these properties are shared by other writers in the tradition if not in the same balance and form that tempts us to consider Propertius and Tibullus together. Catullus at the beginning and Ovid at the end of the classical tradition of romantic poetry indulge the same affinities and a corresponding imagery. Vergil in the *Eclogues* is a troubadour dressed as a shepherd. Even for Horace love is sometimes a rather pastoral phenomenon. And for the influential Gallus, love elegy must have been very much what it is in the elegies of Tibullus and Propertius. We should, in considering the work of Propertius, release him from close association with Tibullus and align him with the general tradition of love poetry in the last three decades of the first century B.C. If we look at them all—Catullus, Gallus (whose works have perished but whose model and formative influence on the others is strongly perceptible), Propertius, Tibullus, Vergil, Horace, Ovid—we see that they form a group of good poets, contiguous in time like the Elizabethans, Metaphysicals, or Romantics of English literary history. They are working to apply and to form a standard sensibility. The result is that the poetry of individual feeling and direct self-expression finds in the words of these artists its most graceful, civilized and subtly modulated Latin cadence.

It is an interesting and decisive development, to which each artist contributes his array of talent and self-conscious energy. The successive poets are conscious of their predecessor's achievements and feel indebted to them; they often hark back to Callimachus or, in general, to the Hellenistic tradition of erudite poetry which he symbolizes. Catullus is epigrammatic and mythological by turns, and most authentically conjures up the "new style" of the *doctus poeta* that all these poets were to explore; his verses ring with the crystal tone of himself, the delighted, capable, suffering artist. Ovid, at the farther end of the sequence, artfully disguises himself in more refined verses, or more conventionally sighs with a sonnet to his mistress' eyebrow. Propertius, midway in the tradition, throbs at being excluded from his mistress' boudoir.

The term "elegy" is elusive. As early as the time of Mimnermus (ca. 630 B.C.), it was the metrical form for love poetry, providing the couplet frame of the long dactylic hexameter and the accompanying slightly shorter pentameter line, and five centuries later Propertius abides by this precedent:

> plus in amore valet Mimnermi versus Homero:
> carmina mansuetus levis quaerit Amor.

"Far more than Homer avails Mimnermus in the realm of love. Smooth are the songs that peaceful love demands." (I. ix, 11-12)

The elegiac meter was also used for martial verse, for dirge and lamentation (the meaning most commonly associated with "elegy" in the modern tradition), and for occasional poetry of a descriptive or topical sort. Horace in the *Ars Poetica* declares that the origins of elegy canot be clearly traced, but in the *Epistle To Florus* he cheerfully assigns to Propertius the role of distinctive elegist in the tradition of Mimnermus. And from the work of the Latin elegiac poets, we can see that elegy as a poetic form provided a vehicle for self-expression, more unguarded than the stately and intricate measures canonically employed by the authentic "lyric poets" (Alcaeus, Sappho, Pindar, Horace). Latin elegy is more like Romantic love poetry than the usual array of ancient lyric poetry is, and offers the artist a chance to break into an expression of individual feeling without abandoning the shape and structure of a definite form and a recognizable standard style. Like the development and articulation of Roman satire as a literary form, elegy became in Roman hands more capable of channeling and distributing materials from the reservoirs of artistic impulses than it had been in Greek literature. Catullus experimented with Latin elegy in this new direction; Tibullus, Propertius, and Ovid expanded and extended elegy to the point where it could virtually serve as a new form, reshaped from its ancient model, and have a future as well as a past.

Significant repercussions of Propertius' success make themselves heard in the lines of two utterly different later poets, Goethe and Ezra Pound. Pound's *Homage to Sextus Propertius,* written in 1917, consists of a group of twelve defiant lyric poems in free verse, "imitations" of the Roman elegist's work, which incorporate themes, subject and whole sections of Propertius transmuted into modern vocabulary and imagery. Through the twelve phases of his homage, Pound vociferously reflects the tone of the "new poet" style, lithely and dramatically vaulting the centuries to find in Propertius the model innovator in an opportune tradition. Pound's translation harps consistently on the individual string:

> Shades of Callimachus, Coan ghosts of Philetas
> It is in your grove I would walk,
> I who come first from the clear font
> Bringing the Grecian orgies into Italy,
>   and the dance into Italy.
> Who hath taught you so subtle a measure,
>   in what hall have you heard it;

What foot beat out your time-bar,
          what water has mellowed your whistles?

Out-weariers of Apollo will, as we know, continue
          their Martian generalities,
          We have kept our erasers in order.
A new-fangled chariot follows the flower-hung horses;
A young Muse with young loves clustered about her
          ascends with me into the aether, . . .
And there is no high-road to the Muses.*

In another version from *Homage,* Pound recreates the celebrated poem wherein Propertius had referred to Vergil's work-
in-progress on the *Aeneid:*

        nescio quid maius nascitur Iliade

Propertius' artistic preoccupations, as he considers the career of
Vergil and casts over in his mind the problems of the epic style
and pastoral conventions, and is driven back to himself and his
addiction to Cynthia; all these personal matters; the insignificant
but unforgettable "facts" of Propertius' individual experience—
are well registered in Pound's version:

Upon the Actian marshes Virgil is Phoebus' chief of police,
          He can tabulate Caesar's great ships.
He thrills to Ilian arms,
          He shakes the Trojan weapons of Aeneas,
And casts stores on Lavinian beaches.
Make way, ye Roman authors,
          clear the street, O ye Greeks,
For a much larger Iliad is in the course of construction
(and to Imperial order)

* This and the following quotations are from *Personae: The Collected Poems of Ezra Pound* (New York: New Directions; copyright 1926, 1954 by Ezra Pound). Quoted by permission of New Directions.

Clear the streets, O ye Greeks!
And you also follow him "neath Phrygian pine shade:
        Thyrsis and Daphnis upon whittled reeds,
And how ten sins[1] can corrupt young maidens;
        Kids for a bribe and pressed udders,
Happy selling poor loves for cheap apples.

Tityrus might have sung the same vixen;
        Corydon tempted Alexis,
Head farmers[2] do likewise, and lying weary amid
        their oats
They get praise from tolerant Hamadryads."
Go on, to Ascraeus' prescription, the ancient,
        respected, Wordsworthian:

"A flat field for rushes, grapes grow on the slope."

And behold me, small fortune left in my house.
Me, who had no general for a grandfather!
I shall triumph among young ladies of indeterminate character,
My talent acclaimed in their banquets,
        I shall be honoured with yesterday's wreaths.
And the god strikes to the marrow.

        Like a trained and performing tortoise,
I would make verse in your fashion, if she should command it,
With her husband asking a remission of sentence,
        And even this infamy would not attract
        numerous readers
Were there an erudite or violent passion,
For the nobleness of the populace brooks nothing
        below its own altitude.
One must have resonance, resonance and sonority
        . . . like a goose.

Varro sang Jason's expedition,
        Varro, of his great passion Leucadia,

1. "Ten sins" should be "ten apples" (Propertius II. xxxiv).
2. "head farmers do likewise" gives a plus-que-Propertian twist to *agricolae domini carpere delicias* (Propertius II. xxxiv).

There is song in the parchment; Catullus the highly indecorous,
Of Lesbia, known above Helen;
And in the dyed pages of Calvus,
                    Calvus mourning Quintilia,
And but now Gallus had sung of Lycoris.
                    Fair, fairest, Lycoris—
The waters of Styx poured over the wound:
And now Propertius of Cynthia, taking his stand among these.

The effusive word-ritual Pound enacts in this collection of
twelve poems "from" Propertius (including the mistakes[3]) is like
a Byzantine mosaic, sharply and chromatically reflecting the holy
wisdom of love's message: spiritual energy is an individual,
unique attribute. The poems in twelve different apostolic attitudes
illuminate, sometimes with an incandescent glow, sometimes in a
harsh and glaring light, but better than criticism can, both how
Propertius' elegies came to be and what they brought into being.[4]
     Another poetic commentator is Goethe, glad to acknowl-
edge and appropriate the influence of Propertius on his own lyric
muse:

> Is it a crime that I was so enthusiastic about Propertius? And
> that the roguish Martial also joined forces with me? That I did
> not just leave the ancients behind to stand guard over the school-
> house? That they came back to life and willingly followed me from
> Latium?
>
> *Hermann und Dorothea,* lines 1-4

3. For Propertius III. iii—"Thou shalt sing of garlanded lovers watching before another's threshold and the tokens of drunken flight through
the night"—
          quippe coronatos alienum ad limen amantes
               nocturnaeque canes ebria signa fugae—
Pound writes with misappropriation:
          Obviously crowned lovers at unknown doors,
          Night dogs, the marks of a drunken scurry . . .

4. It must be noted, in deference to another critical opinion, that Gilbert Highet has denounced Pound ferociously. He calls the *Homage* "an
insult both to poetry and to scholarship, and to common sense." See
Horizon, III (January, 1961), 1: 118.

More formal evidence of the elegiac spirit can be drawn from the *Roman Elegies* V:[5]

> Happy am I now on classical soil, enthusiastic;
> Past and present speak to me louder and more charmingly;
> Here I follow the advice and peruse the works of the ancients
> With busy hand daily, and with new enjoyment.
> But during the nights, Amor keeps me otherwise engaged,
> And even though I'm taught only half as much, I'm doubly grati-
>   fied.
> Am I not learning, by keeping watch over her bosom,
> Allowing my hand to stray down along her side?
> Then do I understand marble better, for I think and compare,
> See with a feeling eye and feel with a seeing hand.
> If I'm robbed of a few hours of day by my beloved,
> I'm rewarded with hours of the night to make up for it.
> We don't just kiss constantly; we have some sensible talk,
> And when sleep overcomes her, I lie awake wrapped in thought.
> Many times I've even composed poems while lying in her arms,
> Tapping out the meter of the hexameter quietly with my fingers
> On her bare back. She breathes, lovely, and asleep,
> And her breath penetrates my breast deep.
> Amor keeps the lamps burning, in the meantime,
> And thinks back over the times when he has performed
> The very same services for the triumvirates of old.

Goethe's ardent research in Rome shows him to be well qualified for the seminar in elegy. The lines wherein he describes himself tapping out the accents of his own future hexameters (his verses are composed in the elegiac meter) on his mistress' flesh constitute a memorable example of new doctrine, romantic fullness of feeling within the limits of classical form. Love and art in such circumstances go hand in hand. One could point to several

5. These poems were written in 1788 and first known as *Erotica Romana*; in 1806 they were published in the collected works of Goethe as *Roman Elegies*.

passages in Propertius where Goethe's scene is pre-ordained in larger essence and with a more pagan candor—the fifteenth elegy of Book II, for example:

> No man more blest! O night, not dark for me,
> beloved bed, scene of such dear delight!
> To lie and talk there in the lamp's soft flickering,
> and then to learn ourselves by touch, not sight—
> to have her hold me with her breasts uncovered,
> or, slipping on her tunic, balk my hand;
> to have her kiss my eyes awake and murmur,
> *Why must you sleep?* and make her sweet demand.
> Shifting our arms, moving to new embraces,
> we kissed a thousand kisses multiplied;
> then, with the lamp re-kindled, fed our senses
> on new delights—the eye is love's best guide.
> For Paris himself, they say, seeing Helen naked
> on Menelaus' bed, loved at first sight;
> Endymion, naked, roused the cold Diana,
> naked to lie with her throughout the night.
> Put on your tunic if you will, my Cynthia;
> these furious hands will rip it into shreds.
>   II. i-xvi, translated by Constance Carrier

Evocative of the art of painting, these lines are embossed with the patina of visual reality, but they shimmer with suggestion. Propertius has an Endymion complex and *wants* to succumb to the lure of the Moon (Cynthia—the sister of Apollo). His mundane love will be bathed in a supernal light. Sleep is an ambivalent force for the artist, who must somehow arouse his impulses and expose them to view, and Propertius likes to write of seeing Cynthia asleep. When in the third elegy of Book I he compares her as she sleeps to Ariadne, to Andromeda, and to a maenad in three successive couplets, he envisages the female attitudes of (1) abandonment, (2) blissful rest, (3) the coiled spring:

Like Ariadne lying on the shore
from which the ship of Theseus sailed away,
or like Andromeda, freed from the rock,
who at long last in softer slumber lay,
or like a Maenad, dizzy with the dance,
flinging herself beside the river-bed,
so did my Cynthia seem the soul of rest,
her slender hands beneath her sleeping head,
So did she seem when I came reeling home,
drunk and disheveled, and the dying light
of the slaves' torches lit the dying night.
                    II. i-x, translated by Constance Carrier

In such passages, the kind of nuclear bits and pieces that may
have triggered Goethe's "enthusiasm," Propertius does not merely
look at his beloved as would a thirsty lover slaking his curiosity.
He sees her as a painter would, and in fact "poses" her, and can
drape his figure with the flowing textures of mythology:

si quis vult fama tabulas anteire vetustas
    hic dominam exemplo ponat in arte meam:
sive illam Hesperiis, sive illam ostendet Eois
    uret et Eoos, uret et Hesperios.

Would you surpass the work of ancient artists?
Paint only her: your fame will reach the skies.
The sight of her would set the East to flaming
and in the West make equal fires arise.
                    II. iii, translated by Constance Carrier

(Perhaps he intends Cynthia to be the first authentically pre-
Raphaelite Madonna.)

Like the alternating lines of the elegiac couplet, Propertius'
assets and liabilities hold his life in balance. Horace and Vergil,
in dire straits, fell into the protective hands of Maecenas and
Augustus and rapidly became official poets on tenure. Tibullus,

was wealthy. As a Roman knight in reduced circumstances, Propertius possessed the margin needed for survival, but he too, after the success of his first book of elegies, enjoyed the benefits of Maecenas' patronage. Almost at the outset, however, he learned what he could do best and consistently refused to step beyond that. Whereas we never quite believe Vergil and Horace when they disclaim lofty ambitions and remark ruefully upon the limitations of their artistic vision and prowess, we consent when Propertius describes the modest sphere of his work. We feel, furthermore, that he expects us to agree with him, just as much as we feel that Vergil and Horace are half-listening for polite murmurs of protest from their audience when they bring up the subject. Propertius was not a great poet: Apollo kept reminding him of that fact and he came to accept it. He was a love poet, riveted to his task by one deeply revealing personal experience, and trained by the exercise of his intellectual curiosity and his esthetic intuition in ways of serving his kind of muse faithfully. He was a good poet—perhaps a more steady and satisfying existence than being a great one—and turned out poems like vases, all alike and impressed with the same authentic style of their maker, yet all different and distinct and handmade. This narrowness of scope is a liability, but it is also an instructive fact of experience for Propertius. His literary knowledge, his education in poetry and speech, is an asset in counter-balance, and its immediately apparent dividend is the deft and versatile use Propertius can make of mythology.

The desire to write, and the Greek example of the crafty and sophisticated Callimachus, invited Propertius to invest and not squander his own talent. Association with the rising generation of literary friends, rivals and acquaintances, was stimulating and provocative for a young poet. Latin itself was coming to the gold standard. A patron like Maecenas, or a statesman like Augustus, augured well for the patriotic native artist. Unpredictable liabilities included: the poet's own precocity; his precipitation into maturity by virtue of the brazen, transcendental love affair with Hostia, whom he was prevented by law from marrying; the concentration of his artistic power in one style; and the restriction of his expression to one principal theme, the course of love in triumph and defeat. But we can hardly fail to say, when we read through the results, that Propertius balanced his experience against his art very winningly, with a mature grasp of the meanings he wished to convey, and a sure touch for defining his objects and imparting to them original grace and color.

Of the four books of elegies Propertius wrote between the ages of twenty and thirty-four, the first is dominantly Cynthia's,[6] the second hers to a large extent. In Book III many other subjects enter so vigorously as to constitute a redirection of his art. Book IV, with its program poem and four others showing the design for verse narratives dealing with Rome's legendary past and ritual customs, its occasional poem on Actium, the felicitous letter of Arethusa to Lycotas,[7] and the glorious solemn eulogy of Cornelia, the deceased wife of Paullus Aemillus Lepidus, which closes the collection, shows Propertius in yet another dimension of his art. Even the two Cynthia poems in this book, the haunting vision of her reappearance to him immediately after her funeral, the gleeful vision of her catching him dallying in inferior company and browbeating him into submission, and the invective poem hurled at the bawd, are in a new vein.

It is clear that as Propertius' art and life progressed he found much more to interest him than the "sole book of Cynthia" had at first indicated. He had fallen in love and learned to chart the course of this spiritual fever, but he had survived the crisis and

6. *Monobyblos Properti*—Cynthia, facundi carmen iuvenale Properti, accepit famam; non minus ipsa dedit. (*Propertius in a Single Volume*—Cynthia, the theme of eloquent Propertius' youthful song, won from him fame; no less she herself bestowed.) This citation is from the *Epigrams* of Martial.

7. ". . . which may have first suggested the epistolary form to Ovid, as the poems on Roman rites and the legends connected with them may have suggested the subject of the Fasti." W. Y. Sellar, *The Roman Poets of the Augustan Age,* I (Oxford, 1891), p. 303.

ended by falling out of love. He learned to judge the experience
sensibly and objectively, when it turned out to be not all there
was to his life and art. Attraction, conquest, submission, quarrels,
reconciliations, the intoxicating loss of identity, and the sobering
rediscovery of self, taught him that love was weightless, baffling
and shifting in its thermal currents:

> Quicumque ille fuit, puerum qui pinxit Amorem,
>   nonne putas miras hunc habuisse manús?
> is primum vidit sine sensu vivere amantes,
>   et levibus curis magna perire bona.
> idem non frustra ventosas addidit alas,
>   fecit et humano corde volare deum:
> scilicet alterna quoniam iactamur in unda,
>   nostraque non ullis permanet aura locis.

> Whoever first portrayed Love as a boy—
> would you not judge his skill beyond compare?
> He saw the lack of wisdom in Love's life,
> the bounty lost because of fretting care,
> and with good reason gave Love windy wings
> and made him flutter in the hearts of men—
> the winds of chance toss men on shifting seas
> and swing them hence and swing them back again.
>   II. xii, translated by Constance Carrier

And as for the rest of his being, why should he not ply his hand
and train his eye on the world and its array of other subjects, corresponding to his *domina* as an Apollo to a twin, one Cynthian
to Another?

> tale facis carmen docta testudine quale.
>   Cynthius impositis temperat articulis.

> your fingers[8] on the lyre might be Apollo's;
> mortal, your music equals the divine.
>   II. xxxiv, translated by Constance Carrier

8. The reference is to Vergil.

A list of the different subjects in Book III alone indicates the variety and range of Propertius' many interests and many choices for composition; the variations away from as well as upon the Cynthia theme in the earlier books are skillful and many. His friends—Tullus, Ponticus, Paetus, Gallus—his sophisticated Rome and its leading literary and political lights, and the mellow, well-defined, enticing Italian landscape, are ingredients for his poems. Larger things can absorb him: death, water, sunlight, nudity, the moon, conjugal steadiness, and Bohemian bachelorhood with its artistic freedom and anxiety. As he writes, Propertius gains a masterly perspective on himself and learns to see what life offers. He is good-humored and resilient, and can redeem his losses by taking stock of what the scene of life can still show him in the way of attractive episodes. Life like art is sometimes to be endured, but it is always distinct and real enough to be thoroughly enjoyed.

Constance Carrier's verse translation makes available for the first time in English poetry the entire result of Propertius' pen. Miss Carrier's choice of alternating rhymes, of exact frames and their deft joining—which one immediately realizes to be her principles of translation in this demanding and delightful poetic re-creation—will remind the reader unobtrusively of Propertius' original achievement in the elegiac style. Her work leads directly, with grace, candor, dignity, and realism, into the world of the once unknown poet from Umbria whose art gave him the power to live on.

PALMER BOVIE.

Rutgers University.
April, 1963

NOTE ON TEXT

The Latin text used for this translation is the Loeb Classical Library edition of H. E. Butler, first published in 1912. The Oxford Classical text of Propertius, edited by E. A. Barber (second edition, 1960) differs from Butler's in the grouping of some of the poems, in the order of some of the lines within several poems, and in some readings (the word to be preferred when the manuscripts vary or seem to be misleading). The following changes in grouping the poems (where Barber's new edition differs from Butler's) should be noted:

BOOK II

Poem xxviii—xxviii and xxviii a in Butler; given as three poems in Barber.

Poem xxx　—in Butler; given as two poems in Barber.

Poem xxxiii—in Butler; given as two poems in Barber.

Poem xxxiv—in Butler; given as two poems in Barber.

BOOK III

Poem viii and viii a—given as one poem in Barber.

BOOK IV

Poem i a—assigned to HOROS in Barber.

It should also be noted that throughout the translations asterisks have been employed to indicate what in the Loeb edition are marked in footnotes as "clearly lost" lines. In most cases the translation is necessarily disjointed at such points.

CONSTANCE CARRIER

BOOK ONE

CYNTHIA PRIMA SUIS MISERUM ME CEPIT OCELLIS...

No girl but Cynthia ever caught my eye
or stormed my heart or felled my passionate pride.
Now love casts down my stiff-necked arrogance,
trampling that neck in his disdainful stride.
And he has taught his captive, loving you,
to hate the shy, to scorn the straitlier-laced,
and give a year of blasphemous love to one
so coy indeed a man might think her chaste.
Tullus, I tell myself Milanion
for love of Atalanta went through hell,
refused no gambit, faced her heartlessness,
and with Milanion finally all was well,
though he had wandered love-sick in the caves,
and wrestled with wild beasts, and once been struck
and left for dead in rock-strewn Arcady—
even Milanion had a change of luck
and won his Atalanta for his own.
O, but for me, love is a dullard, slow,
forgetful of his lore, and lost among
the paths he knew so well, yet does not know.
You priests who ply the necromancer's art,
sorcerers who would steal the moon above,

25

O melt, as I cannot, my Cynthia's heart
by magic; waste her cheek, like mine, with love.
Then will I worship you and do you honor
and praise your powers over streams and stars.
From you too, faithful friends who warn the wayward,
I reach for help as drowning men for spars.
If I could shout aloud my woes, I'd suffer
anything, give my flesh to flame or knife.
Take me to lands past the horizon's rim
and let no woman near to wreck my life.
You, O my luckier friends, stay home and let
your prayers be answered, your unperilous loves
pursue their placid course. For me the nights
are bitter, with no respite from above.
Lovers, I warn you all. Finding one faithful,
keep faith, be steadfast, hold love highly-prized.
Hear me, be warned by me, or else, too late,
learn what I learn now, anguished, agonized.

I. ii

QUID IUVAT ORNATO PROCEDERE, VITA, CAPILLO...

Dear love, dear life, you do not need adorning—
hair curled, silk rustling down your slender side.
Not by that heavy scent, those foreign bangles,
is this your natural beauty magnified.
No. Let that beauty shine in its own brilliance:
your charm, your grace, transcend what gold can buy.
Believe me, art is needless. You are lovely,
and love goes naked nor would trick the eye.
Look at the earth and all that springs forth from it—
how the wild ivy grows, and what more fair?
how the arbutus blooms in hidden places,
and brooks fill channels that no hands prepare;
how the bare shores are rimmed with shining pebbles,
and birds sing sweeter for their lack of art.
No trickery won for Leucippus' daughters
the heart of Pollux, or his brother's heart.[1]
Would Idas and Apollo meet in combat
for a Marpessa decked out like a whore,
Hippodamia ever win by boldness
the prince who whirled her to a distant shore?
Their features shone as clearly as the colors
shine in a picture from Apelles' hand;
they wore their beauty chastely, not desiring
lovers from every corner of the land.
Have I not cause to fear? Yet I am worthy;
honor for any girl is one true love—
and you are doubly honored in possessing
gifts that the gods have shown approval of.
This grace I worship, waking or asleep—
do not defile it. Do not make it cheap.

I. iii

QUALIS THESEA IACUIT CEDENTE CARINA . . .

Like Ariadne lying on the shore
from which the ship of Theseus sailed away,
or like Andromeda, freed from the rock,
who at long last in softer slumber lay,
or like a Maenad, dizzy with the dance,
flinging herself beside the river-bed,
so did my Cynthia seem the soul of rest,
her slender hands beneath her sleeping head.
So did she seem when I came reeling home,
drunk and dishevelled, and the dying light
of the slaves' torches lit the dying night.

Stumbling, I came and stood beside her couch,
drunk, yet not too drunk to be unaware
that love and wine conspired within me now
to drive me to a double madness there.
And so I tried to hold her, rosy-warm
and sleeping, and my toll of kisses take—
quietly, for I know her sudden temper;
I knew how it would rage if she should wake.
Feasting my eyes, I gazed like Argus gazing
on Io's horned head, and smoothed her hair,
and the wreath I had worn laid lightly there.

Apples for your delight: each gift I had
I lavished upon Cynthia whom I love—
placing them stealthily, with hollowed hands,
holding my breath to watch, leaning above,
startled each time you stirred or sighed (although
these were vain terrors) lest your dreaming's course
bring you dark fright, or lest you picture someone—

someone not me—who took your love by force.
But now the moonlight (O officious moon,
trying the window with its lengthening beams!)
wakens her, and with wakening rage she screams,

"Tell me the truth: whose anger, or whose boredom,
has sent you forth from her bed now to mine?
where have you spent the night? whose arms have held you
and left you pale as a ghost and rank with wine?
O may you know the tortures you have taught me;
may you for me that same vain vigil keep—
see my embroidery, see my useless lyre,
how I beguiled the hours I could not sleep.
And while you lay with her, I wept, I wept,
till slumber's kind wings touched me and I slept."

I. iv

QUID MIHI TAM MULTAS LAUDANDO, BASSE, PUELLAS . . .

Bassus, you do your best; your panegyrics
praise every girl but one. I see your game,
yes, but I want no rescue. I am captured,
but my captivity gives me pride, not shame.
Speak of Antiopa and her lovely sister,
of every beauty any age has known—
there's not a man would not judge Cynthia fairer,
Beauty, my friend, is Cynthia's alone.
I tell you she can drive a man to madness
though he no more than look upon her face.
What is my fate, then, I who know her blushes,
her ways to rouse me, her sweet body's grace?
Try if you will—but you will do it vainly—
to break the bonds that make me hers, her mine.
You'll get your punishment. You know her temper.
She'll shrivel you like fruit dead on the vine.
She'll shun you, she'll refuse to let me see you,
she'll call down showers of curses on your head,
there'll be no limits when she starts to gossip.
Bassus, she'll make you wish that you were dead.
She'll pray for your defeat at every altar,
and every god will know how great her wrongs.
Her heart, her pride, would both be roused to fury
should love desert that breast where he belongs.

I am her lover. I will not desert her,
nor wish her changed, nor, please God, ever hurt her.

I. v

INVIDE, TU TANDEM VOCES COMPESCE MOLESTAS . . .

You envy me? you'd have me take you to her?
Well then, let's see where such a path would lead.
What do you hope for, fool? to share my madness?
to rush toward ruin and be wished Godspeed?
to walk through hidden fire, to know all torments,
drink every potion that the devil brews?
She whom you thirst for is not like your light loves:
she has a temper she's not loath to use—
and even if she looks on you with favor,
that too is trouble from the very start;
she will not let you rest, nor your gaze wander;
she'll put an iron padlock on your heart.
A thousand times I'll find you on my doorstep,
rejected, whimpering, all your brave words lost
in gulping sobs, your white face, lined and ravaged,
showing how much this love of yours has cost;
and all that you would say, your vain complaining,
garbled, your own identity unsure.
Then you will know, perhaps, as I, how galling
love's chain can be once it is fixed secure,
and how it feels to find doors locked against you
and nothing left but to slink home alone.
You will not wonder why I'm pale and wasted;
you'll recognize my sorrows as your own.
No use to brag of your ancestral glories—
let be your lineage; love is unimpressed—
but let love even suspect that you are faithless,

your name will lose what power it once possessed.
And when you come to me and ask for solace,
what can I say? My own grief has no cure.
Still, we might share our woes—there will be plenty,
enough for each, of that you may be sure.

You think you can outwit her, Gallus? Never.
Who win her favors pay in hell forever.

I. vi

NON EGO NUNC HADRIAE VEREOR MARE NOSCERE TECUM . . .

I am no ordinary coward, Tullus;
I do not fear the dangers of the seas.
I'd climb the Alps with you as my companion,
or voyage past the far Hesperides.
It's Cynthia's arms have robbed me of my valor;
I hear her weep, I watch her as she pales,
swearing the gods will leave her all forsaken—
I watch, I listen, and my courage fails.
Though she is mine, she will not let me take her;
she screams that if I leave her she will die.
Refusals, threats and tears—these are her weapons.
You could not face them, Tullus, nor can I.
What heart have I for Athens or for Asia?
I'd hear her words, shrieked out, half-heard, wind-snatched
across the widening waters, and I'd see her,
her face all bloodied where her nails have scratched.
You have your uncle's record to surpass, now—
like him the governor, you must seek the good.
You've never loved a woman. What you cherish
is patriotism, justice, brotherhood.
O but that's wise, that's safe, that's as it should be!
Never let loving make a fool of you.
I would not wish an enemy, much less Tullus,
the agonies that Cynthia puts me through.
Fortune has willed it so, that I should suffer,
obedient to the worst she may demand.
Well, men have died for love, they say, and gladly.
I shall be one of that immortal band.
I am not fit for warfare and its glories;
love's is the only war that I can wage.
But you, whatever fortune may befall you,

whatever honors come to you with age—
sea-captain or explorer, merchant, ruler
beloved by all his subjects near and far—
if, in those days, you think of me, remember:
I was born under an unlucky star.

I. vii

DUM TIBI CADMEAE DICUNTUR, PONTICO, THEBAE . . .

Ponticus, sing of Thebes, now; tell its story;
hymn all the horrors of a civil war—
I swear to heaven I think old Homer's glory
descends on you, so fine your verses are.
My song today's no different from tomorrow's;
my range (you're right) is narrower than yours.
I do not serve my wit, I serve my sorrows,
and make a dirge of what my heart endures.
Thus is my whole life spent. This is my measure,
this is my title and my only fame.
No small thing, though, my friend, to offer pleasure
to such a one as Cynthia, all the same.

Though sometimes she may criticize me, lovers
can profit from my words if they'll but read.
The sad heart lifts a bit when it discovers
others have suffered and survived indeed.
My friend, if Cupid's arrow ever finds you—
I pray the gods may spare you such a fate—
you'll try to praise the silken net that binds you,
but these will be new skills, and learned too late.
Then you may seek my songs, and even learn them,
and sigh with lovesick youths above my dust,
His words were truth.
                            Be careful how you spurn them.
Venus' own son may teach you to be just.

I. viii

TUNE IGITUR DEMENS, NEC TE MEA CURA MORATUR . . .

You cannot love me, or you would not go.
Snow-bound Illyria counts more than I?—
and he, whoever he is, you'd leave me for him?
all he needs do is beckon, and you fly?
See from the window how the waves come crashing:
what ship could live when such a tempest blows?
O and that rough wood bunk, and, once you've landed,
nothing but unfamiliar ice and snows.
I pray the gods that every storm be doubled,
or that the Pleiades may never rise,
so that the sailors dawdle by the wharf-side,
and the ropes hang slack, and the faint breeze dies.
Yet I dare not pray thus; the gods might answer,
might wreck the ship that takes you out of reach,
leaving me rooted like a tree, and dying
in impotent rage upon the empty beach.
O my dear love, I cannot wish you evil.
May the gods bring you safe where you would go,
the steep cliffs green and sunlit, without menace,
that northern harbor calm as this we know.
Night after night I'll stand here at your threshold,
bitter in grief, lured by no new love thence;
and every sailor hurrying past—I'll hail him,
crying "What news?" to his indifference,
crying "What port has given my Cynthia shelter?
Tell her," I'll say, although he gives no sign
of hearing, "tell her, no matter what the distance
between us, still I swear I'll make her mine."

                    *   *   *

She hasn't gone! She's promised me! She's staying!
Let those who jeered at me take heed of that!

I've won, I've won, and he, my unknown rival,
has had his answer, had it clear and flat.
Jealous false-friends, no new and northern pathways
will ever tempt from Rome my Cynthia's feet;
Rome and myself she loves: "Without you near me
a kingdom would mean nothing," says my sweet.
My arms will be her home; my bed, though narrow,
will hold us here in love and loving sleep.
Give her the world and put a fence around it,
she'd not be tempted by a bribe so cheap.
Though I had nothing that the world would value,
nothing except the homage of my songs,
and he had wealth and it was hers to squander,
she's chosen me to whom her soul belongs.
I stand here on the highest star of heaven.
Let daylight come now, or let darkness stay—
Cynthia's mine; no other man shall know her.
All days will hold the glory of this day.

I. ix

DICEBAM TIBI VENTUROS, IRRISOR, AMORES . . .

See? Though you mocked him, love has found you out;
no longer do your words ring brash and bold.
O, you have fallen, and before a woman
yours not by love but purchased by your gold.
No priestess knows as well as I what youths
each girl will captivate; I can foretell
her victims by a knowledge dearly bought.
Would I could lose it, and my love as well!
What good is all your pompous rhyming now,
those would-be epics meant to bring you fame?
Love wants no rhetoric, no oratory.
You'll need a softer voice to praise his name.
Put them aside, histories and thesaurus;
sing, if you can, the words of each girl's dream.
You don't know how? O Lord, you cry for water
when you are neck-deep here in love's mid-stream.
I'll warn you further: all your sufferings,
your torments and your pains have just begun.
Wait till at last they've reached their height—hell-fire
would seem delightful by comparison.
Rather a tiger at the throat than arrows
piercing the heart with love's unerring aim!
Watch how you'll weaken, how you'll grant her wishes,
bow to her whim, robbed of both pride and shame.
Still self-deceived, you think you have your freedom.
Love has you on his leash, and pays it out.
By that same self-deception, your possessing
of her will only mask your utter rout.
Once she is yours, she'll be the one to dictate—
you must take up no cause except her own.
This is love's doing—love, all warmth and comfort,

suddenly cold enough to chill the bone.
Whatever you do, flee all that now delights you—
those charms that could melt down the stoniest heart.
What chance against those charms have you, my straw man,
my innocent, what chance against that art?
Confess you're wrong, although it breaks your pride.
Look at love plain and find that love has died.

40

I. x

O IUCUNDA QUIES, PRIMO CUM TESTIS AMORI . . .

My heart at rest, I watched you lose your heart,
Gallus; I even heard your happy tears
the night a girl not Cynthia made my friend
no more the rival every lover fears;
the night I found you in her arms, and heard you
murmur, and heard the words in silence die—
although the moon was half across the heavens,
tired as I was, I could not leave, not I.
What sudden eloquence was in your speech!
How soon you learned the ways that love would teach!

Now, since you've given me your confidence,
take the reward of those who so confide:
first, on my oath I'll keep your sorrows hidden;
second, and better, I shall be your guide.
If she should leave you, I can bring her back;
I'll charm the locks if she should bar the doors;
I'll heal all griefs, no matter how they smart.
What love should seek, what harms and what restores,
Cynthia's taught me, and now, in return
for love's instruction, I shall help you learn.

See, for example, that you do not try
to argue with her when she turns on you;
be neither arrogant nor taciturn;
do with good grace the things she asks you to;
cherish her words when they are kind. And listen—
spurn her, she'll rage; offend her, feed the fires;
but yield and find that you have conquered her.
Then she will grant you all your heart desires.
Freely she's yours if you would not be free,
but you must worship her, and faithfully.

I. xi

ECQUID TE MEDIIS CESSANTEM, CYNTHIA, BAIS . . .

Cynthia, in that town of summer sunlight,
its causeway built, they say, by Hercules,
you lie and bask and watch the dazzling landscape
and feel the warmth poured down upon your ease.
Do you remember me, whose nights are haunted
by memories of other nights? what place
have I still in a heart seduced and stolen
by some vain lover with a handsome face?
If you were safely here, we'd take the rowboat,
with its frail oars, on the familiar lake.
Better to have you here where shallow waters
lap round the swimmers, where the small waves break—
O better so, than that you lie and listen
to his false flattery under that bright air!
A girl unguarded—what's her promise to her?
the honest love that she was proud to share?
I trust you still; I've seen temptation test you—
and yet the tales they tell me of that town!
It is my fear that poisons what I've written;
forgive whatever words may make you frown.
I would not give my mother care more tender;
it is my life your absence would destroy.
You are my sustenance, you are my haven,
the rich unending source of all my joy.
You make my moods: now cheerful, now crestfallen,
I say, "It's Cynthia," and need say no more.
Only come back! leave all that luxury.
Too many hearts have parted on that shore
where modesty and honor lie, and where
true faithfulness is driven to despair.

I. xii

QUID MIHI DESIDIAE NON CESSAS FINGERE CRIMEN . . .

No one in Rome but knows how much I love her,
and none but charges that I do not try—
that if I made the effort I would win her.
How, when these weary miles between us lie?
I have not felt her arms around me,
heard her nor seen her, now, for months on end—
I who was once her pleasure, who, rejoicing
to spend my love, had always more to spend.
Envy has parted us—did a god send it?
was it a magic herb that poisoned love?
You would not know me. Let a woman journey,
and where's that loyalty she assured you of?
Now I must lie alone the night's long hours
and wince to hear my own complaining voice—
happy the man whose mistress soothes his weeping!
Curious, no? how tears make love rejoice.
And happy he who, spurned, can love another—
new bonds can set a broken heart to mend.
Rejected yet not free, I hang in torment.
Where all my joys began, there let them end.

I. xiii

TU, QUOD SAEPE SOLES, NOSTRO LAETABERE CASU . . .

It is your way to mock at my misfortunes,
to jeer at me whom love has left forlorn.
I could not taunt you—I am not so heartless—
if your beloved gave you cause to mourn.
You have a reputation as seducer,
but, though they say you never love for long,
Gallus, I think I see signs that you weaken,
that you find one girl's modesty too strong
for importuning. Here's your punishment
who loved and left so many girls betrayed:
she who will not be kept will keep you faithful.
Yours is a game that's been too often played.
This is not idle gossip, nor mere guessing:
I saw this girl—why should you try to lie?
I saw you as you held her, heard you weeping,
guessed at the words behind your muffled cry.
And I saw more: it shames me to remember.
Your arms were round her like an iron vise—
as foolhardy to try to drag you from her
as any fabled lover from his prize.
You burn for her as Hercules for Hebe,
learning immortal joys on Oeta's height.
One day of such love has effaced all others,
the flame she's kindled burns alive and bright.
Your smugness—she has robbed you of it, Gallus.
and of your freedom, too, taken by storm.
And no one blames you; Jove himself might crave her,
a match for Leda in both face and form.
For all her dignity, she can be charming—
she could cajole the king of men and gods.
You're doomed, you're damned, you'll die upon her threshold.

Use any tactics now, man; what's the odds?
You still may win her, love has changed you so,
and go content where she would have you go.

I. xiv

TU LICET ABIECTUS TIBERINA MOLLITER UNDA . . .

Love is not yours who lie beside the Tiber,
holding the chased cup full of Lesbos' wine,
watching the swift boats skim the river's surface,
the stolid barges move in a slow line,
or glancing now to where the woods' cool shadow
is thick as Asian forests on the hill.
If Cynthia loves these things, she loves me better—
luxury's dear, but I am dearer still.
Too brief, too brief, the nights we fill with loving;
the day's delights—O think no less of them!
the whole world's wonders gathered for our pleasure,
the Red Sea giving up its choicest gem.
And what do kings possess that I should envy?
Kings may well envy me who, till I die,
if fate is kind, will have my Cynthia with me.
It's not true love that kings or gold can buy.
What use would I, without love, have for riches?
Venus can rob a hero of his strength,
can undermine the hardest heart with longing,
can cross a marble threshold, and at length
follow her victim to his bed, cling to him,
and leave him sleepless, white-faced, sunken-eyed.
The sheets may be of silk, the hangings velvet
in all the colors of the rainbow dyed—
I want no such. Uncrowned, I still am king,
having what all men wish for: everything.

I. xv

SAEPE EGO MULTA TUAE LEVITATIS DURA TIMEBAM . . .

How long, how long, I've feared your fickleness—
yet who'd believe that you'd betray me so?
see what new traps are set upon my pathway,
and how unfeelingly you watch my woe—
unmoved, you rearrange your hair, make up
your face, still pale after last night's excess,
and choose your jewels, fastidious as a bride
intent to please him with her loveliness.
Think of Calypso when Ulysses left—
there, on a shore as desolate as she,
how many a day she mourned, her hair unkempt,
and cried her wrongs to the unheeding sea,
sure in her heart that he would not return
but wild to keep alive all that was dead.
And Jason's bride,[2] abandoned, blank with grief,
alone beside the empty bridal bed—
her love betrayed, she would not love again;
if he were false, she would be faithful still.
Alphesiboea, for her husband's sake
avenger, did not hesitate to kill
her brothers, and Evadne, chaste above
all others, died in flames beside her love.

Why do I waste my time in talk of these?
You will not change, though if you would, you might
be my one glorious memory. At least
spare me the vivid phrase that's born of spite;
you need not underline your faithlessness.
Do not provoke the gods you do not heed:
suppose your fortunes worsen—you'll demand
the understanding I so sorely need.

Would I refuse it? Earth would change its pattern
sooner, its rivers turning backward from the sea
to run uphill, the seasons break their order,
before I would deny you sympathy.
Be what you will, but be my own, mine only;
and that wide innocent gaze—let me believe
in that, and in your vows, your protestations
that, witness heaven, you would not deceive.
How can you swear that, when we know you're lying?—
both of us know it; know it was not I
who made you flush and pale, who left red-rimmed
the eyes for whose dear glance I'd gladly die.
No lover will believe me till he must:
Woman's a witch, and worthy no man's trust.

I. xvi

QUAM FUERAM MAGNIS OLIM PATEFACTA TRIUMPHIS . . .

I am the threshold of Tarpeia's house,
and of her good name once the guardian door.
I have let pass great gilded chariots
and felt her captives' tears, but now no more.
Now all around me brawl these drunken louts;
they beat me with their hands all night; they scrawl
obscenities upon me. Torches left
beside me tell their tale to one and all.
I cannot guard my mistress now—I, once
the terror of young men, must take their jeers.
Nothing will change her, nothing gives her shame;
she crowns the evil of all evil years.
And while, almost unhinged, I groan and sigh,
my sighs and groans are echoed and made worse
by him the faithful lover, who is here
perpetually, a taint, a leech, a curse—
berating, blandishing: "O door," he cries,
"cruel as my mistress' heart, as closed to me,
unbar, give entrance to my love, relent,
bear to her ears word of my misery.
No? You will give me nothing, even hope?
nothing except your cold stone for a bed?
Even the night, the turning stars, the winds
pity my faithful and hard-pillowed head.
You pity nothing; men in agony
may die because of you; you give no word.
Let some crack pass my voice through, let it come
to where she lies; O let my voice be heard—
for if it were, if I could reach her ear,
though she is flint, though she is iron and steel,
still I could move her, I could make her melt,

make that unfeeling cruelty learn to feel.
Beyond you, she is happy in his love;
my words are lost on the vague winds of night—
I know this, but it's you who stand between,
stubborn, unmindful of my plaint and plight.
I've never cursed you in a drunken rage—
why do you balk me, let my voice grow hoarse
in vain complaints, leave me disconsolate,
watching the stars move on their steady course?
I've written poems to you, honoring you,
I've knelt and kissed your uncompassionate stone,
worshipped you, and in secret, half in shame,
have left you little offerings for your own!"

I hear him spoil the night and curse the morn.
Both vice and virtue brand me with their scorn.

I. xvii

ET MERITO, QUONIAM POTUI FUGISSE PUELLAM . . .

What else do I deserve, who have left my mistress?
Only the lonely sea gulls hear my cry;
my ship is welcome nowhere, and all my prayers
fall on the coast unheard, fall, fail and die.
And the wind's anger is no less than Cynthia's
if she were here; menacing, how it moans!
O storm without an end, must I meet death
and let these thin sands blow about my bones?
Love, if your voice turned sweet again, and tender,
then the storm's rage were all my punishment.
Can you, dry-eyed, desire my death, nor grant me
a tomb that you might visit? O relent!
I'd give first place in hell to that first sailor
who built the first ship and devised its sail
and found it seaworthy and ventured further.
Who tries to soften Cynthia's heart will fail
(as hard, she is, as lovely), though his courage
would take him to a far and fabled shore,
dark-forested, or send him seeking traces
of other heroes vanished long before.
If fortune let me die in Rome, there ending
both life and love, a stone to mark their close,
then she would weep, her bright hair soft above me,
and lay my bones on petals of the rose;
then she would cry my name over my ashes;
Rest lightly on him, earth, she would implore.
O sea nymphs, save us now; if love has touched you,
spare me, a lover; send me safe to shore.

I. xviii

HAEC CERTE DESERTA LOCA ET TACITURNA QUERENTI . . .

Lonely and silent, here's a place for weeping;
only the West Wind moves among the leaves.
Here I may pour out sorrow, if the bare crags,
lonely themselves, keep faith with one who grieves.
Cynthia, tell me: what has made you scorn me?
when was the first time, Cynthia, you broke my heart?
A month ago I was the favored lover;
now, driven forth, I stand outside, apart.
Do I deserve this? has some magic changed you?
do you suspect I've turned to someone new?
No, no! come back, my fickle one; I'm faithful;
no girl will ever pass this door but you.
I should repay in bitterness my suffering,
yet, when I rage, my anger disappears
lest I should give you reason to be angry
or fill your heart with pain, your eyes with tears.
Or do you think I do not prove my passion
by tell-tale pallor, or an anguished face?
O let me call upon the trees for witness,
Pan's pine tree, or the beech—they know love's grace;
how often they have heard me crying *Cynthia!*
how deep I've carved your name upon their bark!
That doorway where I've wept knows how you've wronged me,
that doorway, closed against me, chill and dark.
When you were haughty, always I was humble,
silent although you stretched me on the rack—
and what return? a bed of rock to lie on,
and broken slumber on this rugged track.
The cries I cannot stifle—sea birds' voices,
screeching and shrill, must drown them all. And yet,
whatever you are, these woods still echo *Cynthia.*
It is your name these rocks will not forget.

I. xix

NON EGO NUNC TRISTES VEREOR, MEA CYNTHIA, MANES . . .

Ah, darling, do you think that death can daunt me?
No longer; funeral trappings hold no fright
for one whose only fear is that you send him
without your love into that endless night.
So deep your image on my eyes is printed
my dust will bear it still, love's lasting mark.
He who died first at Troy[3] could not abandon
his living wife; a ghost, he fled the dark
to seek again what could not be forgotten,
to touch her with his insubstantial hands.
In death I'll have my fame as Cynthia's lover,
for love is worshipped even in those bleak lands.
Think who will greet me!—Trojan princesses
allotted to the Greeks as spoils of war—
lovely indeed, but none so fair as you are,
no other so well worth the waiting for.
Live out your life; I'll wait for you with patience.
Be faithful, make my grave a quiet one.
And yet that very grave, I fear sometimes,
may be a place that you will come to shun,
another love may fade my memory,
and you, though half-unwilling, smile again,
drying your tears—so girls forget their mourning,
admonished and beguiled by living men.
To love you, watch your smiling, hear you laugh—
time without end would be too short by half.

I. xx

HOC PRO CONTINUO TE, GALLE, MONEMUS AMORE . . .

Gallus, my warning's given out of friendship;
do not dismiss it, or be unconcerned.
Fortune can turn against the heedless lover,
as Hercules in distant Mysia learned.
You love a lad as handsome as young Hylas,
as well-endowed as Theiodamus' son.[4]
Take heed, then, wandering past the holy rivers
in Umbrian woods, where Anio's waters run,
along the margin of the Giant's strand[5]—wherever
the waves break at your feet, watch out, I say
There's danger here; the arms of nymphs are ready
to steal the boy, to carry him away.
A dryad's love is warm as any woman's;
if such a love entice him from your side,
your loss will send you searching lakes and mountains
and tracing hopeless paths already tried.
Unlucky Hercules would know your sorrow,
who wept beside the shores of a far land
when from Pagasa's docks he beached the Argo
past Hellen, there on Mysia's rocky strand.
It was a peaceful shore for disembarking;
on the hard ground leaves made soft covering,
and mighty Hercules' beloved Hylas
went wandering off to seek some hidden spring.
The North Wind's two sons, following above him,
caught at him with their hands, bent back his head—

Zetas, Calais, trying to embrace him,
to kiss him, each in turn before they fled.
Swept off his feet, Hylas is carried with them;
he clutches at one pinion; there he clings,
just out of reach, and with a branch he slashes
the closer fluttering of the other wings.
Discomfited at last, the sons of Boreas
leave him. He goes on his appointed way,
still searching for the spring, and, unsuspecting,
comes to the hill stream where the wood nymphs play.
Shadowed by apple trees no hand had planted,
there in the water-meadow flowers grew,
purple and white; he picked them, full of pleasure,
forgetting what he had set out to do;
leaned closer to the stream and stared into it,
enchanted, lost to time, there at the brink,
and finally, bending forward from the shoulder,
cupped in his hands fresh water and would drink—
when suddenly the hamadryads, seeing
all his young beauty, stopped their dance to swarm
upon him lying there, and dragged him helpless
down where dark water closed above his form.
O as they seized him, as he gasped and strangled,
he screamed, and Hercules has heard the scream—
come shouting, pleading, searching. Nothing answered,
only the name, echoed by trees and stream.

Be warned, watch over him, and if before
you trusted these nymphs, trust them now no more.

I. xxi

"TU, QUI CONSORTEM PROPERAS EVADERE CASUM . . ."

Wait, soldier, wait, fleeing your comrades' death,
wounded here at Perugia's bloody wall,
turning your bloodshot eyes, hearing my labored breath—
I was the man beside you through it all.
Save yourself now, escape back to your family,
but hide your tears, nor let your sister know
how Gallus, though he fought free of the enemy,
was by a random spear at last brought low—
for if she find men's bones scattered in Tuscany,
I would not have her guess I perished so.

I. xxii

QUALIS ET UNDE GENUS, QUI SINT MIHI, TULLE, PENATES . . .

Tullus, over and over you ask me, for friendship's sake,
to tell of my rank, my family, my home.
Rome's dead lie in Perugia; Rome's heartbreak
began in Perugia, darkening all of Rome
with the madness of civil war. That soil of Tuscany—
how I hate it, who saw and forever mourn
his body, unburied there, robbed of its dignity,
not even dust for a shroud, naked, forlorn.
There where the Umbrian hills, fertile and fair to see,
slope to the plain below—there I was born.

BOOK TWO

QUAERITIS, UNDE MIHI TOTIENS SCRIBANTUR AMORES . . .

And where do all my love songs rise, you ask me,
and whence the words so sweet upon the tongue?
It's not Calliope, no, nor Apollo,
but Cynthia who's taught me what I've sung.
If you would see her walk, shining and silken,
I'll write a book to tell of her array;
I'll please her, picturing the way those tendrils
of hair, dishevelled, round her forehead stray;
when on the lyre her white hands weave their music,
I'll marvel as they move among the strings.
To watch her drowsing, dark eyes heavy-lidded,
is one more reason why a poet sings.
Our wars of love, waged breast to breast, and naked,
I'll write an Iliad to celebrate.
All that she says or does—what mighty epics
even her merest act and word create!

But O Maecenas, if the Fates had made me
leader of heroes in heroic war,
I would not sing the Titans, nor the pathway
Ossa and Pelion make to heaven's door;
not Thebes, not Troy, the citadel of Homer,

not Xerxes, joining sea to sundered sea,
nor Remus' lands, nor the fierce men of Carthage,
nor Cimbrian threats, nor Marius' bravery.
No. It would be the deeds of godlike Caesar
and of yourself my songs would be about.
And when I spoke of Romans killed by Romans—
Philippi, Mutina—the Sicilian rout—
the ruined ancient hearths of the Etruscans,
Ptolemy's Pharos on the conquered shore,
or when I hymned the Nile that came in mourning
with all its seven streams, to kneel before
great Rome, or sang of kings in golden fetters,
or Actium's prows set on the Sacred Way—
hailing such glories, I would hail Maecenas,
in peace or war Rome's chiefest prop and stay,

* * *

Who does not know Achilles' love, or Theseus'?—
Pirithous, Patroclus, given praise
in Pluto's realm, or high upon Olympus.
And yet Callimachus could find no ways
to thunder forth the wars of Jove and Giant[6]
on Phlegra's plain; and so no more can I
in strict verse tell of Caesar's Phrygian forebears.
As sailors talk of wind and wave and sky,
so each man has his sphere—the soldier's, warfare;
the ploughman's, oxen; and the shepherd's, sheep.
I am no less an expert on my subject:
the love that binds us, waking or asleep.

To die for love is glory; glory also
to love one only; I would have that joy.
Cynthia, I recall, condemns the fickle,
hates Homer's Helen, will not read of Troy.

The cup Hippolytus received from Phaedra
(though in the end it did the boy no harm)
or the strange magic potions brewed by Circe
and no less powerful than Cynthia's charm
which has enchanted me and drugged my senses—
if Jove decree such drinks are mine to drain,
or that Medea heat the cauldron for me—
from Cynthia's door shall move my funeral train.

Physicians cure the sickness of our bodies;
could they cure love, they'd only gain love's hate.
Phoenix, Philoctetes, Androgeon, were rescued
from wounds or even death, by kindly fate.
Telephus, whom Achilles' spear had injured,
was by that same spear's rust again made hale.
But he who rids me of this love could capture
the fruit that Tantalus sought to no avail,
could fill the Danaids' leaking casks with water
and spare their torments; even, with his art,
from that Caucasian crag could loose Prometheus
and drive away the vulture from his heart.

So when I die at last, and nothing of me
is left save on a marble slab my name,
Maecenas, you our greatest boast and envy
whose friendship is my only claim to fame—
if in your carven British chariot you journey
near to my silent dust, O pause beside
that lonely tomb and say, *It was for Cynthia,
for love of heartless Cynthia, that he died.*

II. ii

LIBER ERAM ET VACUO MEDITABAR VIVERE LECTO . . .

When I was free, I thought to lie alone,
but love, for all our truce, has tricked me still.
Beauty like hers—how can it walk among us?
I cannot blame Jove the insatiable.
Fair-haired she is, her hands are long and slender,
her body's ripe, her step is Juno's own,
or like Minerva's at the island altars,
wearing the breastplate that had made men stone.[7]

She is as lovely as Pirithous' bride[8]
whom at the feast the Centaurs stole away;
lovely as Brimo, when in Thessaly
there by the side of Mercury she lay.
Cynthia can surpass you, goddesses
naked on Ida, whom the shepherd saw!
Though she outlive the Sibyl, may that beauty
be one thing time can neither fade nor flaw.

II. iii

QUI NULLUM TIBI DICEBAS IAM POSSE NOCERE . . .

You with your boast that nothing more could hurt you—
you're trapped, your spirit's fallen to the snare.
Now for a month you're sleepless; soon, I warn you,
you'll fill another book with your despair.
I've tried to pass the night in sterner studies—
no use, no use. A fish will drown in air,
a wild boar in the sea. My element
is love; I could not live for long elsewhere.
Yet it was not her loveliness that won me—
although no lily ever grew so white;
her skin is snow just touched with Spain's vermilion,
or on fresh cream a rose leaf lying light—
and not her hair, curling around her shoulders,
nor the two torches of her eyes, as bright
as lodestars, nor the silks she loves to shine in.
I am not caught by any lure so trite.
Not these, but that she dances like a Maenad,
like Ariadne, when the revels close;
that when she sings, or with the harp makes music,
there is no voice, no sound, sweeter than those;
that when she writes, her poetry can challenge
the best that even Corinna could compose.
I think Love sneezed—and what's a better omen?—
when on your day of birth the bright sun rose.
These are all gifts the gods alone have given;
you must not think your mother was the source.
No human parentage could so endow you;
such golden gifts are not in nature's course.
You and you only, born the pride of Romans,
will be of Rome the first to share Jove's bed,
being too fair for gods to leave to mortals—

as fair as Helen was, and Helen's dead.
Why should I wonder that our young men love her?
Troy should have perished for this face instead.
I used to marvel that, for any woman,
cities have fallen, nations warred, men bled.
Paris with his demands, and Menelaus
refusing—now I see that they were wise;
who could do less for beauty? Even Priam
might find war justified by such a prize.
Would you surpass the work of ancient artists?
Paint only her: your fame will reach the skies.
The sight of her would set the East to flaming
and in the West make equal fires rise.
I will not stray from her—should I, Love, stab me
with sharper pain than I have known before.
Like oxen that refuse the yoke, but, slowly
accustomed to it, settle to their chore,
so young men chafe at first against love's fetters,
but then grow calm, enduring more and more,
evil or good; Melampus was imprisoned,
who stole from Iphiclus his cattle, nor
stole them for gain, but out of love for Pero,
the bride he led through his ancestral door.

II. iv

MULTA PRIUS DOMINAE DELICTA QUERARIS OPORTET . . .

What's to do first? Forgive her sins against you;
asking her favor, know you'll be denied;
biting your fingernails, rage at unfairness;
stamp on the ground—but pocket all your pride.
I sleeked my hair (could vanity be vainer?)
and walked slow-paced and straight, to catch her eye.
My ills no sorceress, not even Medea,
could brew a cure for. Here's the reason why:
none sees the cause of it, the blow that's dealt us;
such griefs come to us by a secret path.
We seek no doctor's aid, we need no coddling,
we fear no storm winds or their aftermath,
we walk abroad—and die without a warning.
No man is proof against this love, it seems.
What fortune tellers I have found were humbugs!
How many hags have riddled me my dreams!
A woman's love? My enemies may have it.
I wish my friends the love of some young boy.
From him no griefs; an easy tranquil journey
on little waves that bring no pain but joy.
Him you can soften with a single word;
die, and you leave her cold heart still unstirred.

II. v

HOC VERUM EST, TOTA TE FERRI, CYNTHIA, ROMA . . .

Cynthia, is it true Rome calls you wanton,
true that your name is evil's synonym?
Do I deserve this? In your coin I'll pay you—
leave you and wander at the wind's own whim.
You've taught me that no woman can be faithful,
yet I'll find one my songs can celebrate
who loves me and who gives you all her hatred—
then, my once-loved, your tears will fall too late!
Now when I'm angry, now's the time to leave you—
let rage subside, how soon will love return!
shifting like wind-veered light upon the water
or like the clouds that are the winds' concern.
One word can change to love all anger's landscape.
Now while you're strong, break from your bondage! break!
you'll suffer, yes, but for a few nights only;
endure, and see how slight is such heartache.

But on your beauty, love—swear it by Juno—
of all your lewdness let there be no mark.
Just as the bull's curved horns will gore aggressors,
even the ewe can feel rebellion's spark.
I would not strike you, beat you, tear your clothing,
batter upon your door with my two fists;
I would not seize your hair to jerk your head back
nor bruise your shoulders or your slender wrists.
Such violence is for some boorish lover
who never wore the ivy on his head.
Words are my weapons, and their wounds are subtler—
Lovely she looked, but false was all she said.
Draw yourself up, scorn scandal as you will:
my verse will leave you shamed and hot-cheeked still.

II. vi

NON ITA COMPLEBANT EPHYREAE LAIDOS AEDES . . .

No threshold ever has been thronged like this—
not Lais' in Corinth, where all Greece once bowed;
not that of great Menander's heroine,
Thais, around whom gallants used to crowd;
not even Phryne's, she whose lovers' gifts
could have rebuilt old Thebes and made it new.
And through this doorway pass the ones you say—
and do you lie?—are kissing kin to you.
Jealousy eats me at the sight of them,
their portraits even, even a child in arms,
even your mother and your mother's kiss,
the sister who may sleep beside your charms.
What does not frighten me? I even fear
that so-called sister as a man disguised.
O it was jealousy that fathered war;
out of such evil was Troy's fall devised;
the Centaurs, maddened by Pirithous,
broke the bossed goblets in their passionate rage.
No need to name Greek legends. Romulus,
brute-nursed, bequeathed brute-cruelty to our age.
In all our history, from the Sabine rape,
there's nothing love's forbidden here at Rome.
Virtue's forgotten—yet true happiness
is hers alone who loves her husband's home.
You maids who build to Chastity her temples—[9]
once you are brides, no limit to your lust,
corrupted in once-decent homes by lewdness
of picture or of book; told, *Learn you must!*
May he be damned whose vile sophistications
teach infidelity and mock the true!
Years past, no man would tolerate such foulness

nor wink at such vulgarity, as we do—
we who have left our gods to dust and cobwebs
in grass-grown temples where we go no more.
In such an age, love, how can I protect you
or see that evil does not pass your door?
If you will not be saved, no hand can save you.
O Cynthia, be ashamed of such a life!
Then shall no wife nor mistress steal me from you:
you shall be both my mistress and my wife.

II. vii

GAVISA EST CERTE SUBLATAM CYNTHIA LEGEM . . .

How we rejoiced, my Cynthia and I,
thanking the gods who would not let us part!
The law's repealed at last,[10] that threatening law
that might have riven heart from loving heart,
though Jove himself could not divide true lovers—
could Caesar? Caesar's glorious in war,
but what to love are all his conquered nations?
Cut off my head—I'd rather that far more:
how could I leave this love to wed another,
and, husband to that other, pass your gate
nor turn back, blind with weeping, to this doorway,
knowing my loss, and knowing it too late?
And of what slumbers would those wedding trumpets
tell you? Their sound would turn into a knell.
I shall beget no sons to swell Rome's glory;
not of my sons shall Rome's historians tell.
But let me follow in your camp, my darling,
and I could bridle Castor's mighty horse—
they know me in the wilds beyond the Dnieper,
so my fame grows and widens in its course.
Let me be your one joy; you at my side,
I have no need of sons to feed my pride.

II. viii

ERIPITUR NOBIS IAM PRIDEM CARA PUELLA . . .

She's torn from me, the girl I've loved so dearly
for years—and you, you tell me not to weep?
No enmity but love's can be so bitter.
Kill me—my hatred would not be so deep.
How can I bear to see another hold her?
She was so lately mine; is she no more?
All changes, love not least, with the wheel's turning.
You win, you lose; it's always *either-or*.
The mightiest lords and leaders all are fallen;
the suns of Troy and Thebes are in eclipse
forever. Though for her my gifts, my poems,
I never heard *I love you* from her lips.

II. viii a

ERGO IAM MULTOS NIMIUM TEMERARIUS ANNOS . . .

In all these years that I, too rash, too reckless,
have taken insults from your house and you,
have you once thought of me but as a servant?
done anything but curse me like a shrew?
You are still young, Propertius; must you die, then?
Why not? She would rejoice to see you dead,
though she would keep my ghost harried and haunted,
defile my grave, spoil my poor bones' last bed.

(Why? By the tomb of lost Antigone
lies Haemon, with his own sword in his side,
seeking in death to join her whom he worshipped,
for whom all ties, all hope, he put aside.)

But Cynthia, if I die, you will die with me;
your blood and mine will stain the self-same blade.
This is a shameful debt, but we must pay it,
and not by me alone shall it be paid.

       *   *   *

Even Achilles, with his love lost to him,
lay in his tent and let his weapons rust,
watching, dull-eyed, his comrades dragged to slaughter,
the camp afire, Patroclus in the dust
fallen, his streaming hair blood-stained and matted.
All that might give a heart good cause to break
has left Achilles wrapped in private sorrow,
blind to all else for vanished Briseis' sake—
till her return revived the old Achilles
to drag dead Hector round the Trojan wall.
Not Thetis' son, not armored like Achilles,
what chance have I with love? No chance at all.

II. ix

ISTE QUOD EST, EGO SAEPE FUI: SED FORS ET IN HORA . . .

What he is now, I was, and he, like me,
will be rejected when she tires of him.
Penelope, worth men's devotion, still
is honor's symbol and its synonym.
Remember how she tricked the suitors' pleas
by each day's weaving ravelled out each night.
Hopeless of love's returning, twenty years
she waited for that long-despaired-of sight.
And Briseis, holding close the dead Achilles,
would beat her face with frenzied fist—his slave
who with her tears would wash his blood-stained body
and by the river dig his sandy grave,
ashes upon her head, and strength grief-doubled
to lift his huge frame with her own small hands;
no other there to mourn him—Peleus, Thetis,
lost Deidamia, all in distant lands.
Then Greece was rich and happy in her children;
modesty flourished even in time of war.
But you refuse to spend a night without him—
godless, insatiable—and, even more,
he shares with you your loud and drunken laughter,
your drunken mockery (of me, that's plain)—
he who once jilted you—and you pursue him!
I wish you joy of such a weather vane!
Was it for this, that you should live so lewdly,
I fought death for you, praying at your side,
with all of us who loved you? Where was he then?
what did he care whether you lived or died?
If I had been a soldier sent to India,
or shipped to western seas a world apart,
what tales you'd have contrived! what skilful lying!

No woman ever failed to learn that art.
The shifting tides of Syrtes' gulf are slower,
the leaves the winter winds whip into flight—
nothing so swift as women in recanting,
angered by anything, however slight.
But if this is your way, I yield it to you:
let Love and his attendant throng prepare
their sharpest arrows and in contest pierce me
and send my spirit free into the air.
O let my life blood, flowing, do you honor!
The stars are witness, and the morning frost,
and your door opened for my stealthy entrance,
that, were you mine, I'd count the world well lost.
No head but yours beside mine on this pillow—
if I must lose you, then I'll lie alone.
But if I've served the gods, then, in your loving,
I pray they turn your lover into stone.

*   *   *

As, heedless of their mother's intervention,
the Theban chieftains fought,[11] their swords raised high,
so would I fight with you, though Cynthia pleaded,
and, if you shared my death, rejoice to die.

II. x

SED TEMPUS LUSTRARE ALIIS HELICONA CHOREIS . . .

Time now to pitch it in another key:
to chant the hoof beat on the open plain,
to hymn Augustus and his epic deeds,
to change the lyric to the martial strain.
What though I fail? That I have dared aspire
should be enough. I shall have tried. What more?
Youth sings its praise of love; men, having paid
that debt, as I have paid it, sing of war.
Now I shall walk apart, frowning and grave,
taught by my Muse more somber melodies.
Begin! Abandon all your trivia.
Here is a work to test your energies.
Now Parthia must mourn the Parthian shot,
and Crassus' death, and Parthia's role in it.[12]
India even, bows before Augustus,
and trembling Araby learns to submit,
and every land, to the earth's farthest reaches,
will feel his hand, mighty in peace and war.
I follow in his train—his bard, his singer.
Surely my fate must hold such fame in store.
But those who cannot reach to crown the statue
may lay their garlands humbly at its feet.
So I, not fit to do your glory justice,
offer an incense lowly but still sweet.
I am no Gallus, called to epic heights.
Of love, and only love, Propertius writes.

II. xi

SCRIBANT DE TE ALII VEL SIS IGNOTA LICEBIT. . .

Let others write of your charms, or, love, remain unsung.
No word of praise but falls on barren ground.
Neither beauty nor brilliance, believe me, can outlast
the body lying in its burial mound,
nor any traveler, that tomb unnoted, suspect
what learned loveliness death's hand has downed.

II. xii

QUICUMQUE ILLE FUIT, PUERUM QUI PINXIT AMOREM . . .

Whoever first portrayed Love as a boy—
would you not judge his skill beyond compare?
He saw the lack of wisdom in Love's life,
the bounty lost because of fretting care,
and with good reason gave Love windy wings
and made him flutter in the hearts of men—
the winds of chance toss men on shifting seas
and swing them hence and swing them back again.
And he was right to make Love's arrows barbed,
and sling the quiver ready to the hand:
Love's is an ambush no man can foresee
nor any human breast that wound withstand.
To me he's still the boy whose hurt I bear
but who, shorn of his wings, will fly no more—
here in my heart he lives, and in my blood
wages assiduous and unceasing war.
Why should you choose this shrivelled heart for home?
Shame on you! Seek your conquest otherwhere.
They are fair game who never felt your shaft—
what prize am I, a shadow thin as air?
Yet who would laud you, were that shadow lost?
My Muse is your renown, however slight.
Who else can praise so well my girl's dark eyes,
or say how soft her hands, her step how light?

II. xiii

NON TOT ACHAEMENIIS ARMATUR ERYTHRA SAGITTIS . . .

Erythra was armed with unnumbered Parthian shafts,
but his were fewer than those Love plants in my heart—
Love that has taught me to scorn a trivial Muse
and to learn in the grove of Ascra Hesiod's art.
And this not so that the oaks would heed my words
or wild beasts follow me tamely through the wood,
but that Cynthia may read my verse with delight
and I may reap more fame than the greatest could.

I do not marvel only at what is fair,
nor at the lineage women make their pride.
My joy is to lie in her arms and read to her
and leave that keen intelligence satisfied.
What do I care for the crowd and its babble then?
In her and her cool judgment I am secure.
If she will listen kindly, at peace with me,
there is nothing, not even Jove's anger, I cannot endure.

II. xiii a

QUANDOCUMQUE IGITUR NOSTROS MORS CLAUDET OCELLOS ...

This be the order of the funeral rites
when death has set a seal upon my eyes:
no long procession with its masks of mourning,
no trumpet notes bewailing how man dies;
no final bed with posts of ivory
or cloth of gold; no mourners in a line
bearing sweet-scented platters; only the humble
ways of a poor man's dying—these be mine.
Nothing but three small books as offering,
my greatest gift to Queen Persephone;
and you, your bared breast torn, as my one mourner,
to call my name aloud incessantly,
to kiss the lips that death has made cold marble,
to place the onyx cask of Syrian nard.
Then let fire take me, and my ghost, my ashes,
rest in a tiny urn of clay baked hard.
And let my tomb be shaded by a laurel
when the last flickering of death's flame is done,
and carve these words: HE IS VILE DUST, WHO, LIVING,
WAS FAITHFUL TO ONE LOVE AND ONLY ONE.
As many men will know my sepulchre
as know Achilles' bloody burial mound.
And Cynthia, when death calls you, come—remember!—
by the old path to this remembering ground.
But till that day, love, do not treat me lightly:
not wholly blind or witless are the dead.
I wish that some Fate, kinder than her sisters,
had let death take me as a child, instead.
Why guard the spirit any hour may summon?
Had aged Nestor fallen at Troy's gate,
then he need not have suffered his son's dying,

nor cried, *O Death, you come for me too late!*
Yet you will mourn for me who was your lover:
undying love is due the loved and lost.
When blond Adonis, on the Cyprian mountain,
battled the boar to his own mortal cost,
Venus herself, hair unbound, did him honor
there on his isle. O Cynthia, though you try
to call me back to life, I shall not answer.
What strength have crumbling bones to make reply?

II. xiv

NON ITA DARDANIO GAVISUS ATRIDA TRIUMPHO EST . . .

Not even Agamemnon's joy was greater
when Troy was conquered with its treasure hoard;
not even Ulysses', docking at his homeland;
Electra's, with Orestes safe restored—
though she had mourned what she believed his ashes;
not Ariadne's, when the Cretan snares
were powerless over Theseus. . . . Their rejoicing
is mine. No, mine is greater even than theirs.
Last night has made me king, has made me hero:
make me immortal with another night!
Am I that drooping suppliant she scoffed at,
called a dry pool, made victim of her spite?
Whom does she meet no more with taunts and sarcasm?
who makes her run to do his bidding? I!
How could I take so long to learn her peace terms?
I groan to think of all those nights gone by.
A man in love, as I am, stumbles blindly,
missing the path that otherwise were plain.
Lovers, take heart: such blindness I've a cure for,
an easy formula—one word: DISDAIN.
Cold-shoulder her who scorns you, and, I promise,
in all that you have dreamed of you'll succeed.
Last night how many rivals begged for entrance!
Her head upon my heart, she did not heed.
O greatest victory, I move in triumph,
kings in my train and laurel for my head.
Venus, I pray you, let me deck your altars
and let this verse beneath my name be read:
THESE ARE THE GRATEFUL OFFERINGS OF PROPERTIUS,
WHO FOR ONE WHOLE NIGHT SHARED HIS MISTRESS' BED.

But all's not well yet. Will my ship come safely
to port, or will it founder close to shore?
If any fault of mine should change you, darling,
then may you find me dead before your door.

II. xv

O ME FELICEM! O NOX MIHI CANDIDA! ET TU . . .

No man more blest! O night, not dark for me,
beloved bed, scene of such dear delight!
To lie and talk there in the lamp's soft flickering,
and then to learn ourselves by touch, not sight—
to have her hold me with her breasts uncovered,
or, slipping on her tunic, balk my hand;
to have her kiss my eyes awake and murmur,
Why must you sleep? and make her sweet demand.
Shifting our arms, moving to new embraces,
we kissed a thousand kisses multiplied;
then, with the lamp rekindled, fed our senses
on new delights—the eye is love's best guide.
For Paris himself, they say, seeing Helen naked
on Menelaus' bed, loved at first sight;
Endymion, naked, roused the cold Diana,
naked to lie with her throughout the night.
Put on your tunic if you will, my Cynthia;
these furious hands will rip it into shreds.
You'll have bruised arms to show your mother, sweetheart;
when did frustration ever cool hot heads?
Youth's in those light ripe breasts, not yet gone flabby
as women's do when they have borne a child.
O let us love until we are each other—
we on whom Fate these few swift hours has smiled.
It will not be for long. A night will take us
which must refuse to brighten into dawn.
Strain closer to me, lock me in a nearness
that will not fail when time would have it gone.
Remember doves, how they are one in passion,
yoked, as we are, the male and female one?
Love is a frenzy, and it has no limit;

no love, if it is true, is ever done.
Let earth bear winter fruit and shock the farmer,
or let the sun god drive the steeds of night,
rivers run backward, or the seas be shrivelled,
fish dead in unaccustomed air and light—
these things will chance before I love another.
Living, I'll praise her; dead, dream of no other.

A single year of such nights, should she grant it—
for this I'd give up all three-score-and-ten.
If there were many, I would be immortal;
if there were even one, a god again.
Ah, men are fools who do not pass their life so,
limbs languorous and heavy with much wine.
Did they, there'd be no need for swords and warships,
for sailors' bones to steep in Actium's brine;
no need for Rome to break her heart when Romans
die in the shambles of a civil war.
No god was ever outraged by our wine cups—
men can say this for us, if nothing more.
Do not renounce life while its light is in you.
Given all your kisses, still I'd have too few.
See how the withering wreath lets fall its petals
to float within the cup—O Cynthia, you
and I are lovers blest and hopeful, but
who knows what day may see that last door shut?

II. xvi

PRAETOR AB ILLYRICIS VENIT MODO, CYNTHIA, TERRIS . . .

That praetor from Illyria, fat with money—
to me he's trouble, but to you he's prey.
Could he have drowned upon his voyage hither,
Neptune, what gifts I would have brought your way!
Now feasts are spread, but I'm not there to share them;
nightlong, but not for me, the door's ajar.
You're not the fool who'd fail to reap this harvest,
to clip this ram—your shears, how sharp they are!
Then when you've stripped him to the hide, dismiss him,
nor even turn to see which way he went.
Cynthia's unimpressed by robes of office,
but she can guess men's wealth to the last cent.
Venus, I pray you, let his lecherous pawing
fail into impotence, and let him rot.
O, is it true, then? anyone can buy her?
is every girl corruptible? Jove, say not!
She cries for jewels—I seek them at the sea's edge;
presents from Tyre she'd have me bring her home.
I wish that every Roman were a pauper
and a thatched hut the finest house in Rome!
Then there'd be no bought love—there'd be no money.
A man could watch time change his mistress' face.
You would not leave my bed six nights of seven
nor take so foul a man in your embrace.
And this though I'm still faithful—you're my witness!
To teach a woman loyalty is vain.
Whenever that foreign lout comes lusting for you,
you make him king where once I used to reign.
Her necklace brought despair to Eriphyla;
Creusa died in burning agony—
your cruelty should have burned away my weeping,

yet my grief dogs your vices constantly.
I've had no wish for months to see the theater,
or eat, or seek the friends I used to know.
I could beg shame itself to give me freedom,
but shame's a word forgotten long ago.
I think of Antony, and the strangled groaning
of his lost legions there at Actium drowned
when he turned back his fleet for love of Egypt,
hunting a shelter never to be found.
Such victories are Caesar's fame and glory;
the hand that conquered sheathed the sword in peace.
O Jove, let that barbarian and his presents,
the clothes as costly as the golden fleece,
the yellow-gleaming chrysolite, the emeralds,
be lost in storm, washed up on empty sands,
or turn to dust and water as she holds them.
Jove is not deaf to perjured love's demands;
his justice knows forsaker and forsaken.
You've heard his thunderbolt run through the air,
you've seen his lightning leap across the heavens.
They're not the Pleiads' or Orion's care.
Lightning is made for punishment, not plaything,
and with it Jupiter will blast the girl
who's false in love, like her who once betrayed him.[13]
What of your dresses stitched with gold and pearl?
will they and all your baubles keep you warm
or brave, when you must face the South Wind's storm?

II. xvii

MENTIRI NOCTEM, PROMISSIS DUCERE AMANTEM . . .

If you must lie to me about your lovers,
beguiling me, my blood is on your head.
Each night of solitude I sing my sorrows,
lying alone—and you in what man's bed?
Pity poor Tantalus, waist-deep in water
that shrinks whenever he would quench his thirst;
or Sisyphus who strains to push the boulder
up the long slope, and fails. Pity these cursed,
but pity even more the piteous lover—
lover with whom no wise man would change place.
I, once the king admitted and admired,
for ten days now I have not seen your face.
Bitch! I should find a rock, a cliff, to leap from,
or mix a poisonous drug and drink it down.
I cannot hurl my words at that closed doorway,
nor wander weeping through the moonlit town.

Yet I can't leave her, though I try it often.
Seeing how true I am, may she not soften?

II. xviii

ASSIDUAE MULTIS ODIUM PEPERERE QUERALAE . . .

Too much complaining kindles only disgust in many.
Suffer in silence, and, so, bend her will to your will.
Whatever things you have seen, swear you have not seen any.
Cover the wound and deny that the knife had power to kill.

II. xviii a

QUID MEA SI CANIS AETAS CANESCERET ANNIS . . .

Suppose that I were withered and white-headed,
my forehead furrowed and my cheeks deep-lined?
So was Tithonus, yet Aurora loved him,
nor let him lie alone as day declined.
There where she lives, beyond a waste of waters,
she kissed him as she left to bring the dawn,
driving her fresh-washed horses, and, returning,
lay in his arms until the day was gone—
even then not ready to rise, calling the heavens
unjust, begrudging the earth its morning light.
As great her joy in Tithonus, old and immortal,
as her grief for Memnon, dead in the Trojan fight.
She felt no shame to have so aged a lover,
fondling his wrinkled face and his white hair.
But you resent it, that I am yet a young man—
having yourself not too much time to spare.
Still, I can shrug, remembering that Cupid
to those whom once he blessed can bring despair.

II. xviii b

NUNC ETIAM INFECTOS DEMENS IMITARE BRITANNOS . . .

What's this new fad of painting like a Druid,
of covering your face with foreign dyes?
Beauty is best when left as nature made it;
that Belgian rouge is foul to Roman eyes.
There is a special room in hell, I swear it,
that's set aside for those who tint their hair.
Leave all such nonsense; in my sight you're lovely,
and will be while you're faithful, that I swear.
Look—if some fool appears with bright blue eyebrows,
must we despise all eyebrows not bright blue?
You have no son, my darling, and no brother;
I would alone be brother and son to you.
Sleep in your own bed and be safe from scandal,
don't show yourself with make-up on your face.
Now then take care, for I'll believe all rumors—
there is no speed that these cannot outrace.

II. xix

ETSI ME INVITO DISCEDIS, CYNTHIA, ROMA . . .

Though I can hardly bear to let you leave me,
thank God you leave me for a little town
where there will be no chance of new seducers
whose flatteries will wear your virtue down;
where men will fight no brawls beneath your window
nor shout your name to break your midnight dream.
Live there among the good back-country farmers
and learn how beautiful are hill and stream.
There'll be no gambling table to corrupt you,
nor the temptations of a city shrine.
You'll see the oxen, patient at their ploughing;
you'll watch the skilful sickle prune the vine;
you'll carry incense to the rustic altar
where humble peasants sacrifice a kid;
and if you join the dance, bare-legged, with them,
no city man will spy from where he's hid.
And I will be a huntsman, and I'll worship
not Venus, no, but at Diana's fane.
I'll catch wild beasts, and nail upon the pine tree
their horns, my prize, and give the hounds full rein.
No lions, though; I know my limitations;
and no wild boars to put my speed to shame.
A rabbit, now—that might be fitting quarry,
or birds, brought down by my unerring aim
through groves where old Clitumnus shades the waters
where the white cattle stand knee-deep at noon.
And O remember, sweet, I shall be with you
between the waxing and the waning moon.
No woods, however lonely, and no rivers
wandering through the thick-mossed hills, but hear
how I call out your name, over and over.
What does the absent lover dare not fear?

II. xx

QUID FLES ABDUCTA GRAVIUS BRISEIDE? QUID FLES . . .

Why do you weep like Briseis for Achilles?
Why do you weep like lost Andromache?
You're mad. You weary heaven with your complaining
that I'm untrue, that there's no faith in me.
No mourning dove is shriller in Athens' woodland,
such floods of tears not even Niobe weeps
beside the twelve tombs on the Phrygian mountain,[14]
her tears a river down the mountain steeps.
Though Fate should bind my arms in iron fetters
or lock me up like Danae in her tower,
I'd break the bonds, I'd leap the wall to reach you;
if you should call me, love would give me power.
Men tell lewd stories of you—I do not listen.
If I can trust you, you must trust me, too.
I swear upon my mother's grave, my father's—
may their ghosts haunt me if I lie to you!—
that till the dark shall take me, I'll be faithful.
One love be ours, death the same day at last.
Your name, your beauty—were these not sufficient,
the lightness of your yoke would hold me fast.
For seven long months now, Rome's streetcorner gossip
has linked your name with mine, and all those nights
over and over again your door's been open,
your bed has offered me all its delights.
Yet have I bought these pleasures? Never. Never.
It was your kindness, sweet, that let me in.
I, whom the woman all men seek has chosen,
can I forget how generous she has been?
If I forget, let hell's own Furies plague me,
let me know hell's worst torment for my own—
punishment worse than Tityus with vultures,

or Sisyphus with his eternal stone.
So! No more notes, accusing and beseeching.
My love from first to last is yours alone—
not rashly offered and not rashly ended.
What lover's claim could be so well defended?

II. xxi

A QUANTUM DE ME PANTHI TIBI PAGINA PINXIT . . .

May Venus damn him for his lies about me—
Panthus, who never spoke a true word in his life!
You've learned today my talents as a prophet:
Panthus, who loved you so—he's found a wife!
O, all those wasted nights! For shame! Look at him,
happy while you, his dupe, must lie alone,
and he and she talk of you, and he tells her
how you pursued and marked him for your own.
I swear he lives to brag about his conquests—
husbands are valued for that kind of thing.
So Jason as a stranger tricked Medea
to wed the daughter of another king;[15]
Calypso, unbelieving, watched Ulysses,
that treacherous Greek, spreading his sails for flight.
A girl's a fool who will not learn the lesson:
BE SLOW TO LOVE, SO MANY LOVES ARE LIGHT.
And have you learned it? No! This new contender—
can any man alive deceive you still?
do you trust him and not trust me, who, early
or late, adore you, near, far, well or ill?

II. xxii

SCIS HERI MI MULTAS PARITER PLACUISSE PUELLAS . . .

I've played the field impartially—you know that,
Demophoon—and paid for it in woe.
There isn't a street in Rome I haven't wandered;
the theater trapped me, too, and long ago.
O those white arms flung out, that white throat pouring
its music forth to win my willing heart!
and that same trouble-seeking heart still conscious
of this one's bare breasts, or of that one's art
that makes the hair fall careless on her forehead
or catches up her curls in some new way.
God, how I suffered if her glance went through me—
I'd still burst out in cold sweat to this day.
Does that susceptibility seem curious?
You say, *But why?* I cannot tell you why.
Men gash their limbs with knives—and for what reason?
What frenzy's there? I do not know, not I.
But every man is given a vice by nature:
mine—this is simple—is to be in love.
It's a sixth sense, this feeling for all beauty,
a sense that blindness could not rob me of.
I'm thin? Nonsense! I never have felt better.
I flourish in these bonds that hold me fast.
I'll tell you frankly, many a girl has found me
still eager when a night of love has passed.
Jove, for Alcmena's sake, made the stars slumber,
and for two nights left heaven without a king;
yet the third day his godhead still was mighty.
Love is the bird with an unwearied wing.
Achilles, when he left the bed of Briseis—
was he less terrible to his enemies?
and was he less a hero in the battle,

that prince whose love was all Andromache's?
Consider them and me: small choice between us,
save that they fought for Mars and I for Venus,

Even the sky has sun and moon for lovers;
why then should I be satisfied with none?
So this girl's faithless, so she won't receive me—
I'll find a dozen more before I'm done.
So that girl feels I've used her badly? Let her!
I've any number who will let me in.
Twice safe the ship that has a double anchor,
and half the worry if the child's a twin.

II. xxii a

AUT SI ES DURA, NEGA: SIN ES NON DURA, VENITO! . . .

If your heart's flint, say *No;* if it would yield, then come.
Let's not waste words; it's one thing or the other.
What woe in the world is worse than doubt to suffer from?
No man but fears she's left him for another.
O how he sighs and tosses on the rumpled sheets of his bed,
his mind's eye seeing her welcoming his rival!
Even his slave's worn out, pressed to tell what's being said,
though it ruin the last faint hope of love's survival.

II. xxiii

CUI FUIT INDOCTI FUGIENDA HAEC SEMITA VULGI . . .

I hated well-worn paths, and would not walk them—
I, who would drink now from the public well!
I even bribed another's slave to find her
and, coming back, tell what she had to tell.
Shameless, I begged him, *Is it through the Campus
she strolls, or through a shaded portico?*
Then, when I've gone through hell-fire, comes her letter:
What presents have you brought? she wants to know.
Or I must face her guardian who hates me,
or lie in hiding in some filthy hut,
waiting the single night when I shall have her.
What price the privacy of doors that shut!

Here, on the other hand, comes another type, now—
an easy stride, head bare, a cheerful sight.
She has no guardian, and her shoes are muddy,
but she's a ready partner for a night.
She will not chatter; she's not apt to nag you
to give her all your father's grudging loans.
She won't say, *I'm afraid; get up now, leave me;
my husband's near; I feel it in my bones.*
I'd rather give an honest whore my loving
than play this vulgar hole-and-corner game.
Love is the loss of liberty. Who'd love, then,
if he must lose his honor in love's name?

II. xxiv

TU LOQUERIS CUM SIS IAM NOTO FABULA LIBRO . . .

Your book's successful, and the whole town's talking
of you and Cynthia, now; how do you feel?
Who would not sweat a little at such phrases,
modestly—or from love he should conceal?
Yet all these puritans would not condemn me
if there were still fire in this love affair;
no one would look upon me as seducer
were we too deep in love to know or care.
So it's no wonder that I seek streetwalkers—
no slander there. You think that doesn't count?

*   *   *

She wants a fan made out of peacock feathers,
a crystal ball to keep her fingers cooled;
ivory dice she wants (I lose my temper),
and cheapjack bangles from the Sacred Way.
I laugh at such demands—but this I can't bear:
to be the laughingstock I am today.

II. xxiv a

HOC ERAT IN PRIMIS QUOD ME GAUDERE IUBEBAS? . . .

Was this the hope you gave at love's beginning?
Why must you be as fickle as you're fair?
One night, two nights, together, and you tell me
to leave your bed—that I'm not welcome there.
A little while ago you praised my love songs,
and now—so soon!—your love's gone who knows where.

I'll match this man in wit and poetry-making—
once he gives up divided loyalties.
Sweet, if you choose, send him to fight the Hydra
or steal the fruit of the Hesperides,
drink poisons gladly, or, shipwrecked, sea water,
suffer for your sake hideous miseries.

(Test me, my darling, test me with such labors!)
He'll prove a coward from the very start
who with his boasting blinds you to the weakness
that will, before the year's end, make you part.
But my devotion will outlive the Sibyl,
and death itself will find you in my heart.

You'll close my eyes then, murmuring, *Propertius,*
rest now, who were beyond all others true.
No man more faithful, though you had no title,
and no great wealth, like his, would come to you.
Nothing that you can do will ever change me.

What if I suffer? That is beauty's due.
Many a man has loved your loveliness,
loved it, and lingered—yet now all are gone.
How briefly Theseus stayed with Ariadne!

How soon poor Phyllis lost Demophoon!
Medea rescued Jason, yet he left her
only a bitter crust to live upon.

Hard is the heart that can feign love for many,
that would parade itself for many eyes.
I am a commoner, and poor—but who else, tell me,
will mourn your beauty when that beauty dies?
Yet I would rather have that beauty mourn me,
calling my name in little broken cries.

II. xxv

UNICA NATA MEO PULCHERRIMA CURA DOLORI . . .

Loveliest woman born, and burden of anguish
for me whose fate forbids the word *Return!*
my books shall leave you famous beyond all others.
(Calvus, Catullus, make this your concern!)
Old soldiers sleep without their rusted weapons;
oxen, grown old, refuse to pull the plough;
the wrecked ship rots on the seashore, and old armor
hangs on the temple walls, unhandled now.
Let me outlive Tithonus, outlive Nestor;
love will not dwindle or be dwarfed by age.
Better to let the great bronze bull of Perillus
burn me, the victim of some tyrant's rage;
better to let Caucasian vultures tear me,
to let the Gorgon stare me into stone.
I will not break, though flint's worn down by water,
and rust takes sword and scabbard for its own.
But no closed door can ever daunt a lover
if he is steadfast and unmoved by threat.
Disdained, he pleads, says his was the wrongdoing,
and seeks the path that wisdom would forget.
You, poor young fool, so proud at love's full tide, now—
learn that a woman's faith is swift and short.
How can the sailor hope to keep a promise
when his sea-shattered vessel limps to port?
how can the prize be claimed by any runner
before the seventh lap around the goal?
The winds of love blow soft; you must not trust them.
Storms may come late, but they will take their toll.
And meanwhile, if she loves you, do no boasting—
keep that joy hidden in your silent heart.
Your own words' echo, once the love is over,

will leave the deepest wound, the sharpest smart.
And though her door is open, enter seldom:
whatever's envied does not long endure.
I'd be as you are now, though, were this era
not one to mock such words as *true* and *pure*.
Corrupted by the age, still I am faithful—
each man must choose the path that he would tread.
But you who argue safety lies in numbers
will come to grief each time you turn your head—
on the one hand, a blonde girl to delight you;
a dark one, on the other; both are fair;
here is a Greek, with grace to make you marvel,
and here a Roman, both beyond compare.
Clad in the cheapest clothes or born to the purple,
each is fit means for Cupid and his plan.
Remember the sleepless nights his arrows give you!
One woman is trouble enough for any man.

II. xxvi

VIDI TE IN SOMNIS FRACTA, MEA VITA, CARINA . . .

Heart of my heart, I dreamed I saw you shipwrecked,
I saw your weakening hands clutch at the air;
I heard you gasp that you had done me evil;
I saw you dragged down by your brine-soaked hair,
and tossed like Helle on the purple waters—
Helle, who slipped from ram's back into sea.
And terror shook me lest your name be given
that gulf, and sailors mourn your memory.
I prayed to Castor and Pollux, prayed to Neptune,
to mortal Ino now immortal made—
but in my dreams your flailing arms grew feeble;
your voice that called my name—I heard it fade.
If he had seen your eyes, the sea god Glaucus,
he would have seized and kept you for his own.
How envious they would have been, the sea nymphs,
their loveliness surpassed by yours alone!
But as you sank, I saw a dolphin swimming,
Arion's lute bearer, your guide to shore,
and I, prepared to leap and die beside you,
felt terror fade, for I could bear no more.

II. xxvi a

NUNC ADMIRENTUR QUOD TAM MIHI PULCHRA PUELLA . . .

Cynthia's mine! At this let all men marvel,
and through the city let my fame be spread!
Though emperors seek her and though Croesus beckon,
she will not turn a poet from her bed.
She says she scorns all wealth, having my verses—
no woman ever reverenced poetry more.
True hearts are constant; he who wins by bribing
may have a hundred light loves at his door.
Sail to Cathay, sweetheart, and I shall follow—
we're one, and the same breeze shall fill our sail,
the same shore give us rest, the same tree shade us,
the same spring quench our thirst and never fail.
Who cares how narrow is the bed we lie on,
whether it's at the ship's prow or the stern?
I can bear anything, even though storm winds force us
far from our course, with small hope of return—
like those that drove Ulysses to disaster
and wrecked the Greek fleet in the angry seas,
or those that carried Jason north, a white dove
guiding him through the cleft Symplegades.
May Jupiter himself kindle our vessel
so long as you remain within my sight!
and if we drown, may the waves take my body,
but on yours, washed ashore, the earth lie light.
Who frowns on love like ours? Not Neptune, surely,
who was, in love, the equal of heaven's king:
Amymone lay with him in the meadows
when he had pledged the drought-worn land a spring—
and, having had her, he redeemed his promise:
a golden urn poured forth the magic stream.
And Orithyia, ravished by the North Wind,

would not condemn him, brutal though he seem.
O we could tame even the monster Scylla,
could even charm Charybdis into rest!
No clouds shall mask the stars that ride above us—
Orion's path be clear from east to west.
And if death find me on your body lying,
where would I find a worthier way of dying?

II. xxvii

AT VOS INCERTAM, MORTALES, FUNERIS HORAM . . .

Men, alive for an hour, would know that hour's ending,
would learn the path by which their doom draws near;
on the unclouded sky they search, like the Phoenicians,
what star to trust in and what star to fear.

Whether we fight the Parthians on foot, or sail to Britain,
death may be waiting us on sea or land.
A man in civil war, caught by opposing armies,
can feel the rock he stood on turn to sand.

Fire comes in the night, swallowing and engulfing;
into the cup what poisons find their way!
Only the man in love is proof against such terrors:
he knows his doom, its source, its kind, its day.

Though he has taken his place at the oar on death's black river,
though he looks at those sails of which no man can tell,
if he hears the voice of his mistress, calling him back from
    that kingdom—
let heaven thunder, he'll fight his way from hell.

II. xxviii

IUPPITER, AFFECTAE TANDEM MISERERE PUELLAE . . .

Look, she is dying—help her, Jupiter! save her!
her death would be chalked against you as a crime.
These are the days when the air itself is scorching
and the earth glows red-hot now, in the Dog star's time.
Yet in all truth it's neither heat nor heaven
that makes her suffer: it is her godlessness.
Hers is the fate of the bold ones, the defiant
whose words have the weight of the wind, or even less.
Or is Venus vexed that you have been called her equal?
You know her jealousy of all that's fair.
Have you offended Juno in her temple?
sniffed at Minerva's eyes? You would not dare.
Beauty was never sister to discretion.
This is the failing that has made you ill.
Surely by now you've had your share of sorrow;
presently peace will come, I know it will.
Io, by Juno's vengeance made a heifer
drinking Nile water—she is deified.
And Ino, after all her years of wandering,
becomes Leucothoe, the sailors' guide.
Andromeda escaped the grim sea monsters
to find reward as Perseus' faithful wife,
and the Arcadian boar that was Callisto
now as a star saves many a sailor's life.
If the fates mark you for the dark eternal,
the fates of funeral made blest for you—
tell Semele the dangers beauty's heir to;
she whom Jove loved and killed will know them true.
Of all the heroines of Homeric legend,
you, by consent of all, will have first place.
Meet death with all the reverence you can summon—

at the last moment death may turn its face,
and jealous Juno pardon you your beauty,
grieving that death should touch so fair a head.
The savage music and the chanting cease now;
the laurel's burned, the altar fire's dead;
the night bird shrills an omen in the darkness;
the moon's unmoving and a devil's spell.
Old Charon's boat will take our loves together,
slow-moving through the sluggish pools of hell.
Pity her passing, Jove—and me who loves her.
She lives, I live; she dies, let me die too.
Grant me her life, I'll do you every honor,
and write, SHE LIVES ONLY BY GRACE OF YOU.
And every day, by your decked altars kneeling,
she'll chant the sorrows that have known your healing.

II. xxviii a

HAEC TUA, PERSEPHONE, MANEAT CLEMENTIA, NEC TU . . .

Pity us mortals, O Persephone!
Lord Pluto, soften the heart that all men fear.
there are so many beauties in your kingdom—
may we not keep this girl, our loveliest, here?
Iope's yours—Europa, white-skinned Tyro,
Pasiphae, who bore the Minotaur,
the fairest Greeks, the loveliest of Trojans—
Apollo's Troy, old Priam's, now no more.
And Roman maidens as delectable—
these too are ashes on a funeral pyre.
No face can charm death and no fortune buy him;
all must fall victim to his greedy fire.
O Cynthia, rescued now from equal dangers,
dance to Diana, show your gratitude;
pay homage to the goddess once a heifer,[16]
and for us both give thanks ten times renewed.

II. xxix

HESTERNA, MEA LUX, CUM POTUS NOCTE VAGARER . . .

Last night I wandered drunk along the roadways,
and with no slave to catch me if I fell—
when small boys swarmed around me. I was frightened,
too frightened to count them—why, I cannot tell.
Some carried little torches, some had arrows,
and some had fetters ready for the limb,
and all were naked. One, more arrogant, shouted,
"Now seize him! We have all been warned of him—
he is the one that woman was denouncing"—
and then a rope circled this neck of mine
and my tormentors closed in, with one yelling,
"Death to the man who says we're not divine!
You don't deserve it, but she's waited for you,
while you, you fool, sought for another's door.
Her hair escapes the purple ribbon that binds it,
her eyes, sleep-heavy, search for you once more.
She lies in all the fragrance of Arabia,
or in the greater fragrance made by love.
Spare him, now, brothers! he has given his promise;
we'll take him to the house we're guardians of,
and give him over into her safekeeping.
Henceforth stay home when all sane folk are sleeping."

II. xxix a

MANE ERAT, ET VOLUI, SI SOLA QUIESCERET ILLA . . .

At dawn, and wondering who was last night's lover,
I entered—and I found her all alone!
alone and never lovelier, even in purple
praying before the Vestals' altar stone,
telling her dreams there to that virgin goddess,[17]
lest any ill luck threaten her or me.
So fair she was, wakening from fresh slumber,
her beauty unadorned for me to see.
"What in the world?" she said. "So! You've come spying?
You think my ways untrustworthy as yours?
I'm not so easy. I will take one lover—
you or a new man, if his love endures.
No mark on this bed of another's body,
no sign that two have lain upon this bed.
You do not find me breathing hard or blushing—
you'd know if I'd been false to you," she said.
I would have kissed her, but she held me off, then
jumped up and slipped her sandals on her feet.
I haven't had a happy night since that one,
but that's the fate that spies deserve to meet.

II. xxx

NUNC TU, DURE, PARAS PHRYGIAS NUNC IRE PER UNDAS . . .

Have pity on me—must you make this voyage?
what's there to seek around the Caspian Sea?
You must be mad. Flee past the Don, or further—
still Love will hunt you down relentlessly.
There's no escape, though Pegasus should bear you
cloud-high, though Perseus' wings be on your feet;
even with Mercury's sandals, no escaping
through the cleft air. Your rout will be complete.
Love flutters over your head and every lover's;
Love is a burden keeping the proud neck bowed.
He never sleeps; his eyes are on you always—
you'll never lift yours, once he has you cowed.
Yet if you disobey, you can appease him.
You must be prompt, though, in your penitence.
Stiff-necked old men—let them denounce our pleasures;
we'll walk our way with royal indifference.
Their deaf old ears hear only ancient precepts
where we would listen to a pipe well-played—
the pipe once flung in the river by Minerva
whom her puff-cheeked reflection had dismayed.
Should I feel shame who serve one mistress only?
That's criminal? then let it be Love's crime.
Do not accuse me. There are cool caves, Cynthia,
in green hills where we'll while away the time,
where we can see the crags the Sisters[18] cling to,
singing of those fair women Jove preferred:
how he took Io, how he burned for Semele,
how to Troy's towers he flew once, as a bird.[19]
(But if no man has ever withstood Love's weapons,
why charge me with a guilt all men must share?)
You must not shock the grave and holy Vestals—

though they are chaste, Love is not unknown there,
if it is true the Muse Calliope
bore Orpheus to a disguised Apollo.
And when you stand there foremost in the dance
with Bacchus and his practiced wand to follow,
then will I wear the sacred ivy wreath.[20]
Without you, all my words and wit grow hollow.

II. xxxi

QUAERIS, CUR VENIAM TIBI TARDIOR? AUREA PHOEBI . . .

Why are you late? you ask me. I've watched Caesar
open Apollo's golden colonnade[21]—
enormous; columns of red-streaked yellow marble,
and, in between, the Danaids displayed.
And in the center rose the marble temple,
dearer to Phoebus than his Delian home.
And all the doors were carved of Libyan ivory,
and the Sun's double chariots stood on the dome.
One door showed how the Gauls were hurled from Delphi,[22]
and one how Tantalus' daughter came to die.[23]
And finally, with Leto and Diana,
the god himself, in flowing robes, on high,
more beautiful than even the living sun god,
singing with silent lyre and lips of stone,
and round about the altar, carved by Myron,
four cattle, almost living flesh and bone.

II. xxxii

QUI VIDET, IS PECCAT: QUI TE NON VIDERIT ERGO . . .

He sins who sees you—seeing is desiring;
therefore the blame is all upon the eyes.
Why do you seek the oracles of Praeneste?
why should you go to Tusculum otherwise?
why should you drive to Tivoli so often,
or to the south along the Appian Way?
Why will you not stay here when you're at leisure?
Friends tell me not to trust you. *Fool!* they say,
Look at her rushing frenzied to the altars,
worshipping Trivia by the torches' light!
You hate the colonnade of Pompey, shadowed
with columns, and with golden curtains bright;
you hate Rome's avenues, bordered with plane trees;
you hate the nymph-filled waters rising here
from Maro's statue, pouring through the roadways
to the carved Triton, there to disappear.
You think you hate these, but that's self-deception—
it's not the city, it's my eyes you flee.
In vain, in vain—and all your wiles are useless;
your tricks are all familiar now to me.
But for myself, no matter. When you've lost it,
that's when you come to value your good name.
You're what they whisper of and gossip over—
wherever I go in Rome, it's still the same.
Yet was it ever otherwise with beauty?
Scandal appears as soon as beauty's seen.
And it is true none claims that you work with poisons—
of this Apollo knows your hands are clean.
So if you've spent some nights in wanton pleasures,
such are your ways; I'm not upset by them.
Tyndareus' daughter ran off with a stranger,[24]

but was brought back, and no one to condemn.
And think how Mars was lusted for by Venus![25]
Yet for this none in heaven call her cheap.
Mount Ida still recalls the nymph Oenone
who lay with Paris there among his sheep,
while old Silenus and the hamadryads
looked on, and Dionysus watched as well,
and with them Nais, gathering wild apples,
her hands upstretched to catch them as they fell.
Among such sinners, none would ask of this one,
Who keeps her? who provides her with the best?
O Rome, these days you have your greatest glory
when one girl's found who does not ape the rest!
What Cynthia does, Lesbia did before her;
surely the follower is less to blame.
Only a newcomer would think our morals
and those of the old Sabines are the same.
You could more easily dry up the ocean
or pull the stars down with your mortal hand
than you could change our taste for what is sinful.
Sin's been the rule since Saturn ruled the land,
the fashion since the flood that spared Deucalion—
and since that flood, tell me, what bed is chaste?
what goddess ever lay with one god only?
Think of the white bull Minos' queen[26] embraced,
of Danae imprisoned in her tower—
what could she do but yield to Jove's assault?
If your life's patterned, then, upon these ladies',
live freely. Who's to say who is at fault?

II. xxxiii

TRISTIA IAM REDEUNT ITERUM SOLLEMNIA NOBIS . . .

Once more these dismal rites have come to plague us:
for ten nights Cynthia's at the sacrifice.
This ceremony[27] Io brought from Egypt
for Roman women—damn it twice and thrice!
Whoever the goddess was who parted lovers,
a bitter one indeed she must have been.
And yet you, Io, whom Jove loved in secret—
you found a hundred paths to wander in
when Juno set those horns upon your forehead
and turned your soft voice to a bellowing roar.
How often in your stall would strawberry branches
and oak leaves—food, now!—make your poor mouth sore!
But now that Jove's redeemed you from your penance,
have you grown haughty, back in human guise?
must you have more than Egypt's adoration?
why must you come for Rome to idolize?
Why for your sake should women sleep alone nights?
Touch finger to your forehead, after a while,
and find horns sprouting out. O leave our city!
The Tiber has no fondness for the Nile.
But, Cynthia, since my griefs have gained your pity,
let us make love three times for each lost night . . .
You do not hear. You let my words slip by you
while Icarus' oxen wheel the stars toward light.
You drink unwearied; midnight does not move you;
if you're bored by the dice, I see no sign.
To hell with him who first invented vineyards
and ruined wholesome water with his wine!
If it was Icarus, they did right to kill him,
those Attic farmers to whom he gave the grape.
Eurytion the Centaur died of drinking;

for Polyphemus wine left no escape.
Wine ruins beauty; wine can spoil love's summer;
wine leaves the best-beloved unrecognized . . .
What good are sermons? Look, your hand is steady;
with wine your beauty's only emphasized—
your rose-wreathed head bending above my verses ,
your voice speaking the words quiet and clear.
Let the whole table drown! drain the decanters!
spill them into the gold cups waiting here!
No woman's bed is by her own choice lonely;
love marks the goal toward which all men must strive;
the restless heart swings toward the absent lover.
It is not constancy keeps love alive.

II. xxxiv

CUR QUISQUAM FACIEM DOMINAE IAM CREDAT AMORI . . .

Never entrust to Love your lovely mistress.
I trusted mine, and almost she was lost.
Believe me, there's no man but covets beauty,
and none is true. I learned it to my cost.
Love breaks up friendship and can leave kin hostile;
love can turn amity to feud and strife.
Who was it Menelaus welcomed? Paris.
Medea fled her home, a stranger's wife.[28]
Lynceus, could you dare to touch my Cynthia?
Devil! Your hands should have been powerless!
What if she is fickle, unfaithful to me?
Could you have lived and faced your faithlessness?
Kill me—but honestly, with sword or poison—
kill me, so long as you leave her alone.
You may still be my comrade when we're old men;
here, take my fortune, everything I own
except for her; share anything but Cynthia—
I'd not have Jove himself as rival there.
I am so jealous I fear my own shadow;
my own suspicions chill the summer air.
There's only one excuse for you to offer—
say you were drunk. This—this I could forgive.
Don't try to take me in with moralizing;
we learn love's value every year we live.

* * *

Love, after all these years, sends Lynceus reeling.
I'm glad at least that now our gods are his.
What good is Socrates and all that wisdom
that tells us why the world is as it is?
What use are all those old Athenian lyrics?
Your ancient poets are no help in love.
If you must sing, then take, if not Philetas,

Callimachus to make a model of.
Tell what Achelous bore for Deianira—
that river who would rival Hercules;
or how Meander turns and twists through Phrygia,
helpless within its vast complexities;
or how Adrastus' famous horse Arion
spoke at the games for dead Archemorus—
your fate is still that of the Theban Seven,
of Capaneus, of Amphiaraus.
Don't strain your gifts toward Aeschylean verses:
listen to softer rhythms; sway with those.
Shape out your poems on a narrow anvil,
melt your hard heart with your own fiery woes.
Homer, Antimachus—no man moves safely;
beauty will use its power to the full.
The farmer uses goad and yoke and harness
before he plows an acre with the bull.
I'll have to tame your spirit for the hardships
that love requires lovers to endure.
You'll win no girl by showing how the world moves
or how the sun's course keeps the moon secure;
she will not ask who's judge for our hereafter,
or if the lightning's given conscious aim.
Consider me, inheriting no fortune,
bearing no title of ancestral fame:
watch me at banquets; listen to the brilliance
that girls admire—and you make light of this!
Languid, I lie among the fading rose wreaths,
a mark for love his arrows never miss.
Vergil[29] does honor to Apollo's Actium
and to the honors that great Caesar bore;
Vergil can breathe new life into Aeneas,

founding our race on the Lavinian shore—
Vergil, unequalled among Greek or Roman!
Beyond the Iliad's thunder hear it rise,
that other music, telling of the pine woods,
singing the shepherd song that never dies.
With a milk-fed kid, or even a dozen apples,
a country girl, he says, may well be won.
Happy the man who thus can tempt a sweetheart!
Tityrus would praise so virginal a one.
Who would not envy Corydon, loving Alexis,
his master's favorite boy, fresh-cheeked and young?
The wood nymphs prize him, though he drops his reed pipes
in weariness, and leaves his song unsung.
Vergil, like Hesiod you depict the country—
where the wheat grows, and on what hill the vine;
your fingers on the lyre might be Apollo's;
mortal, your music equals the divine.
No man has read your songs who does not love them,
whether he lives as rakehell or recluse.
You are the swan whose least note is pure lyric;
Anser, that poor hack—Anser is a goose.
My themes are all men's. Varro wrote of Jason,
but Varro's love songs—these are what will live;
and passionate Catullus gives to Lesbia
more fame than all the wars of Troy could give;
by love and grief Calvus has kept undying
his dead Quintilia's name; and, dead as well,
Gallus, heartbroken by the cold Lycoris,
still bathes his wounds in the cold streams of hell.

Fate, mark me as you marked these men, that I,
making my Cynthia deathless, shall not die.

BOOK THREE

III. i

CALLIMACHI MANES ET COI SACRA PHILETAE . . .

Callimachus, may your spirit make me welcome;
let me enter the grove of Philetas, his arts to learn.
I come like a priest from a place of crystal waters;
I give my Roman themes a Grecian turn.
Under what trees did you spin the thread of your music?
to what song did you dance? what fountains cooled your thirst?
Down with the man who would busy Apollo with warfare!
Let the rhythms run smoothly—but they must be polished first.
Such poems as these have given me my triumph:
the Muse, my daughter, rides behind garlanded steeds;
cherubs cluster around me here in my chariot.
Who follows it? every Roman who writes or reads.
Loosen your rein if you will—to compete is useless.
The path to the Muse is a strict and narrow way.
Men may sing of Rome and add to her glory,
praising her every conquest—well they may!
But the pages I bring down from the Muses' mountain[30]
I bring by a road no other man may tread.
Make delicate wreaths, O Nine,[31] at your sacred fountain.
I would not have a weighty crown for my head.
What I have lost in life because of men's envy
shall be repaid in death by a doubled fame.

115

Then the quick years will make all things seem greater;
then men will remember the almost-forgotten name.
Else who would know of the wooden horse at Troy's gateway,
or the river god[32] who wrestled with Hercules?
Who would have heard of Simois or Scamander,
or of Hector dead—who would have heard of these?
Troy itself might forget the Trojan heroes
and Paris, too, the fated source of its woe;
and that same Troy that Hercules twice conquered
might have died with none to care, none even to know.
Homer foretold its fall, and, ages later,
new generations give him new acclaim.
Your sons, singing of Rome, shall cite my verses—
I can predict my own posthumous fame:
Behind my bier a reverent Rome shall follow.
So am I promised by my lord Apollo.

III. ii

CARMINIS INTEREA NOSTRI REDEAMUS IN ORBEM . . .

O let us sing again, then, as we used to—
Cynthia, let old songs bring new delight.
Wild beasts, they say, were tamed by Orpheus' music,
and rivers halted in their headlong flight;
music induced the rocks of Mount Cithaeron
to roll to Thebes and form into a wall;
and Galatea reined her sea-wet horses
near Aetna's shore, at Polyphemus' call.
No wonder, since I'm favored by Apollo
and Bacchus, every girl is at my feet.
My house is plain; it has no ivory vaulting,
no marble columns; I cannot compete
with the orchards of Alcinous; no grottoes
of mine are watered by the Marcian stream.[33]
But I am Muse-befriended; all men read me;
Calliope does not weary of my theme.
Happy the girl who is that theme—you, Cynthia;
none shall forget the beauty I have praised.
Not Jove's own house at Elis, rivalling heaven,
nor the Pyramids, so slowly skyward raised,
not even Mausolus' tomb with all its riches
can outwit death, or know a happier fate.
Fire may burn, rain strip them; they will crumble
under the years' intolerable weight.
But from remembered genius, fame shall flower.
It is only wit that death does not devour.

III. iii

VISUS ERAM MOLLI RECUBANS HELICONIS IN UMBRA . . .

I dreamed I lay in Helicon's soft shadow,
beside the fountain struck by Pegasus;
and, growing bold, I felt my powers able
to sing our kings most high and glorious.
I drank at springs that Ennius had drunk from—
however unworthy, there I quenched my thirst,
like him who told old tales of civil warfare
and of Aemilius and the foe dispersed;
of Fabius delaying, and of Cannae
where good men's prayers for aid have proved their use;
of Hannibal defeated by our Lares
and Jove saved by the cackling of a goose.[34]
But from his grove (I dreamed) Apollo spied me
and turned and spoke, leaning upon his lyre:
"What are you doing here? O hopeful hopeless,
now to what heights does vanity aspire?
Fame will not come to you from such, Propertius.
In meadows your small chariot should be found.
Your books are all for girls, and girls may fling them
in boredom or impatience on the ground.
Your subject's circumscribed; do not exceed it—
so much your skiff will hold, but nothing more.
Keep one oar in the sand and one in water;
stay in the shallows; let the ocean roar."
He pointed with his quill at a small dwelling;
a fresh path led there through the moss-grown floor.
Here was a green cave, walls all lined with pebbles;
and timbrels hung there from the hollowed stone;
there were the instruments the Muses play on,
Silenus' statue, reeds that were Pan's own.
Those birds I love to watch, the doves of Venus,

dipped their red bills into the Gorgon's spring,
and here and there the Muses moved, their soft hands
busy with gifts allotted them to bring.
One sang to the lyre, a second gathered ivy,
a third twined roses with deft-fingered care.
And suddenly one laid her hand upon me—
Calliope, I think, she was so fair.
"You'll be content," she said, "to let swans draw you;
no war horse speed you to the battle plain.
You shall not sound a war cry on the trumpet
that blood should leave upon the earth its stain.
Nor shall you heed the wars of Marius' making,
nor care if Rome beats back the German horde,[35]
nor see the Rhine choked with the mangled bodies
of those who, as they lived, died by the sword.
No. You must sing of rose-wreathed lovers watching
before another's door, of drunken flight;
your songs must urge the lover to assail him—
the man who keeps a fair wife out of sight."
These were her words; my lips she touched with water
of the spring wherein Philetas found delight.[36]

III. iv

ARMA DEUS CAESAR DITES MEDITATUR AD INDOS . . .

On Parthia now Caesar our god plans warfare;[37]
through the pearl-bearing sea[38] he makes his way.
Romans, there's much to win; once Tiber triumphs,
then the Euphrates moves beneath its sway.
Not easily nor soon is Parthia conquered,
yet it will be. The gods of Parthia's world[39]
will know the Roman Jove. War horses, ready!
ships trained for war, set forth, your sails unfurled!
The omens favor us. Avenge dead Crassus!
Add to Rome's history its brightest page.
O father Mars, O fateful fires of Vesta,
let me live on into that golden age
when cheering crowds surround and halt the chariots
piled high with all the loot such prowess wins.
Lying in Cynthia's arms, I'll read the records
of captured towns, and see the javelins
that horsemen hurl, the bows of trousered fighters,
the captured chiefs under the captured spears.
Venus, protect your race! Aeneas' grandson,
Caesar, uphold that heritage through the years!

To those that won the spoils the spoils belong.
I, on the Sacred Way, offer them song.

III. v

PACIS AMOR DEUS EST, PACEM VENERAMUR AMANTES . . .

It is Love as a god of peace we lovers worship;
wars with a mistress are all that we would make.
It is not for golden loot that I am hungry;
I have no thirst that a ruby cup might slake;
not for me need the oxen plow Campania;
of the bronze from Corinth's burning[40] I have none.
It was intransigeant earth, Prometheus, that you moulded,
the heart too carelessly, too quickly, done!
The body made, he left the mind neglected,
and, worse, the soul he should have valued most.
So, for such lack, we're tossed on endless oceans,
seek out new foes, make fighting all our boast.
And yet what booty can we take past Lethe?
We're carried naked to the ship of hell.
There Marius and Jugurtha sit together;
victor from vanquished there no man can tell—
no man tell Croesus from Ulysses' beggar.[41]
Yet a full life may find death not unkind:
Helicon I have worshiped from my boyhood,
and in the Muses' dance my hands have twined.
So let me drink of his wine to honor Bacchus,
and wear a wreath of roses every day—
then when at last I'm impotent and aging,
when my black hair is thinned and streaked with gray,
I'll be content to turn to other matters—
learning what wise god rules this part of earth;
how the great horned moon waxes, wanes, and rises
returned out of its dying to rebirth;
and where the winds spring up that sweep the ocean,
and what the East Wind's seeking with his blast,
and how the clouds draw their unfailing water,

and what day for the world shall be its last;
why the bright rainbow swallows the rain water;
what made Mount Pindus in Epirus quake;
why the sun's horses went in dark-robed mourning,[42]
or why Arcturus should so lately wake
and with what close-set fires the Pleiads glitter;
what force restrains the sea upon the shore;
why the full year has always its four seasons,
and whence the snake wreath that the Furies wore;
if gods rule underground, or giants suffer,
Phineus fasts, Alcmaeon flees his fate—
if there is rock, or wheel, or lake-bound thirsting;[43]
if triple-headed Cerberus guards hell's gate;
if Tityos is cramped, if folklore's nonsense,
and past the funeral fire no terrors wait.
Such is my end. Fame's followers, wait upon her,
and rescue Crassus' banners from dishonor.

III. vi

DIC MIHI DE NOSTRA, QUAE SENTIS, VERA PUELLA . . .

Tell me, Lygdamus, what you think of Cynthia—
speak as a man, and not as Cynthia's slave.
Should I believe you? were they lies to cheer me,
have they been falsehoods, the reports you gave?
The man who brings a message should be honest—
and how much more a slave, who lives in fear!
Tell me again; begin from the beginning—
everything you remember I must hear.
How when she weeps? for you have watched her weeping,
half-hidden by her hair's dishevelled strands.
Was there no mirror on her couch, Lygdamus?
no bright-jewelled rings upon her slender hands?
was it a somber robe that she was wearing?
her rouge, her make-up—were they put away?
was the house sad, the women-servants quiet,
and she among them, knitting the hours away?
and did she use the wool to stanch her weeping
over the words I spoke so bitingly? . . .
"So this is his reward? You heard his promise—
perjury is a crime for slave or free.
How can he leave me so, give me no comfort,
take to his house a woman I would not name?
It gives him pleasure to see me thin and lonely—
if I were dead, he'd mock me still the same!
She's caught him not by love but by black magic!
her witchcraft makes a puppet out of him.
Love philters full of bramble-toads and serpents
she's brewed, and filled the goblet to the brim—
toads, serpents, owls' feathers found in cemeteries.
She's shaped wax images and muttered spells.
Now bear me witness: he'll come crawling to me

and I'll have vengeance. So my dream foretells—
over his empty bed the webs of spiders,
and she false to him even in his embrace."
O if she spoke these words, and spoke them truly,
go back as fast as you can, your path retrace;
tell I send her, with my tears, this message:
Love, prey to anger, keeps its honor still.
A dozen nights I've had no other woman;
my heart no less than hers the same fires fill.
If peace can follow after such a quarrel,
Lygdamus, you'll be free, I swear you will!

III. vii

ERGO SOLLICITAE TU CAUSA, PECUNIA, VITAE . . .

Money—it's love of money that is fatal;
for money's sake men die before their time;
money is cruel; it nourishes men's vices;
it is the source of woe, the seed of crime.
Money, for your sake Paetus sailed to Pharos
and in a sudden raging gale was drowned—
poor Paetus, dead so young, and by your doing;
fallen where giant fishes circle round.
His mother could not give his body burial
among his kin, that decent last respect—
he has the sea birds now to be his mourners;
the sea entombs him with the ship it wrecked.
O Boreas, who stole Orithyia,
what loot would you have won from such a lad?
Neptune, what joy for you in such disasters?
men better than he no country ever had.
O Paetus, drowning, did you trace your life span?
call on your mother? Who would hear? No use:
Neptune is deaf. From rock to ship were cables—
the storm saws through them, and the ship's torn loose.
Now that you have his life, give earth his body;
drift over, cover him softly, idle sands.
"Even the brave must fear," the sailor murmurs,
pausing a while where Paetus' tombstone stands.
Go, build your curving keels, build death's own weapons.
Such death could come but from the hands of men.
Earth's not enough for death; we give him oceans.
See how men's craft betrays them once again.
Home could not hold him—how then could the anchor?
What's his reward who finds his land too small?
All that he makes, the winds will take for plaything;

no keel grows old; no harbor welcomes all.
What is the sea? a path to lure the greedy—
for one who wins, a thousand others fail.
The shores have seen how Agamemnon, grieving
over Argynnus drowned, refused to sail,
though all the fleet was massed there for departure—
and so for this was Iphigenia slain.
And Nauplius burned false beacons on the headland
to avenge his son and make Greek triumph vain.
Ulysses one by one has lost his comrades;
his wiles were powerless against the sea.
Had Paetus stayed to plow his father's acres
with his father's oxen, had he heeded me,
he might feast now before his household altars—
poor, but at peace, and living strong in hope.
He could not bear to hear the storm winds howling;
he was not made to strain at oars or rope;
his should have been a room of Chian marble
with a down couch on which to rest his head—
yet the wind ripped the nails from his slight fingers;
he gulped the waters that met overhead.
A plank upheld him for a few wild moments—
so many ills combining for his death!
And at the last he cried to the black waters
that even then strangled his gasps for breath:
"You gods of the Aegean, winds that chill me
and waves that pour their weight upon my head,
what is my crime that you should want to kill me?
I have not lived—why should you wish me dead?
On rocks where sea gulls nest, my body's battered—
Neptune, I feel your trident's angry blows.

There are the shores of Italy; let my mother
find what is left of me cast up on those—"
But as he cried aloud, a twisting eddy
sucked up his desperate breath, and so he died.
You, Thetis, daughter of that selfsame Ocean,
you should have caught him up, been at his side;
you Nereids might have held him above water—
he was no heavy burden for your hands.
North Wind, you shall not tear my sails to tatters.
Safe with my love, I seek no distant lands.

III. viii

DULCIS AD HESTERNAS FUERAT MIHI RIXA LUCERNAS . . .

O what a quarrel last night's lamps looked down on!
how you railed at me, how you stamped and cursed!
till, pushing back the table, you flung the goblet
full of a wine that could not quench your thirst!
Keep on—with doubled fists, rage! Tear my hair out,
with pointed nails threaten to scar this face,
to burn my eyes within their very sockets,
rip at my clothes, leave not a fold in place!
You could not show me better that you love me;
this reckless wrath can only prove your love.
All women are the grovelling slaves of Venus
who call down imprecations from above;
who past their jealous lovers walk well-guarded,
or Maenadlike go reeling through the crowd,
or from their frantic dreams awaken trembling,
or at a rival's portrait cry aloud.
I've watched these torments, and I've learned their meaning;
I know that they are true love's surest sign.
No love is lasting if it's free of quarrel.
Grant girls of spirit to all friends of mine!
and let those friends see where her teeth have marked me—
let my dark bruises prove she's been with me.
I'll hug my grief or hark to your lamenting;
my own tears or else your tears I would see—
tears for the secret notes written with effort,
for words you write you would not dare to speak.
I scorn the sighs that cannot break through slumber;
let Cynthia's anger pale my wasted cheek.
What fire stirred Paris when through the whole Greek army

he came and in the arms of Helen lay!
While the Greeks won, while valiant Hector struggled,
love's private war was still the greatest fray.

I'll wage unending combat, with or for you.
Give me no peace, no rest, love, I implore you.

III. viii a

GAUDE, QUOD NULLA EST AEQUE FORMOSA; DOLORES . . .

Rejoice because you are fairest! You would grieve
were you less than that, but your pride is not misled.
And as for him and the snares that he would weave,
may his in-laws meddle long after they should be dead.
It was anger at me that made you give him leave
(if ever you did) to lie one night in your bed.

III. ix

MAECENAS, EQUES ETRUSCO DE SANGUINE REGUM . . .

Maecenas, son of the kings of Tuscany,
if you would keep the fortune that you prize,
let my song launch itself on seas less ample;
canvas too widespread makes a boat capsize.
What good to lift a burden that's too heavy,
drop it in shame, take ignominious flight?
All men have different tastes and different talents—
the palm's not given at a stated height.
Lysippus makes his statues all but living;
Calamis' horses all but breathe and race;
Apelles wins his fame by painting Venus;
in miniatures Parrhasius holds first place;
Mentor takes groups of men and moulds their figures;
for Mys, acanthus blooms make harmonies;
Jupiter done in ivory—that's by Phidias;
in Cretan marble—that's Praxiteles.
Some race victorious chariots at Elis;
some in the foot race seek their fame instead;
one's made for peace, another shines in warfare—
each has a bent to which he's born and bred.
But I, Maecenas, by your own example
I'll vanquish you, your precept as my guide.
Though you place where you will, O wise lawgiver,
your axes, symbols of imperial pride;
though you could pass among the Medians' weapons
or fill your home with the picked spoils of war;
though Caesar gives you strength, and though your fortune,
the more you spend it, seems to grow the more—
you stay behind the scenes, you seek no honors,
of your own will you haul your canvas down.
But fame unsought will make you our Camillus;

your modesty will win the more renown,
and you will walk at the right hand of Caesar;
your loyalty will be a household word.
Oceans are not for me; my skiff will loiter
on little streams, by little breezes stirred.
I shall not sing the seven fights,[44] nor Bacchus
whom Jove snatched from the Jove-burned citadel;[45]
nor of the Scaean Gate, nor the returning
of the Greek ships that tenth year[46] shall I tell,
nor of burned Troy, broached by that horse of Pallas,
its god-built walls razed by the Grecian plow.
Say that Callimachus would like my verses
for their Greek turn—that's praise enough for now!
For boys and girls let me be love's first herald;
let them pay me as god all godly rites.
I'll sing, you leading, of love's arms, and giants
fighting on Phlegra's plains or heaven's heights.
I'll tell of Rome's first kings, the twins wolf-nurtured,[47]
the walls of Rome established, Remus slain,
the Palatine with Roman cattle grazing—
what glories, you instructing, I'll attain!
I'll celebrate your all-triumphant chariots,
the shafts of those false Parthians who fled,[48]
Pelusium's camp conquered by Roman power,[49]
and Antony, by his own doomed hand dead.
Give me your favoring nod; take up the guide rein,
cheer me, whatever rank my efforts get.
Your praise is all my boast: let men say of me
I follow the example you have set.

III. x

MIRABAR, QUIDNAM MISISSENT MANE CAMENAE . . .

I marvelled when I woke to find the Muses
around me in the rosy light of dawn.
This was their message—that it was your birthday.
Three times they clapped their hands, and they were gone.
O let this be a cloudless day, I pray them,
the wind, the wave, unmoving on the shore;
let me see no one on this dear day weeping;
may Niobe's mournful stone shed tears no more;
may even the sea birds this day stop their screeching,
and Philomela cease to mourn her son.
And you, sweetheart, well-augured, waken early.
Do for the gods all things that should be done.
Wash sleep from out your eyes with crystal water,
and round your finger curl your shining hair;
put on the dress you wore when I first saw you,
and on your head—a wreath of roses there.
And pray such beauty never may diminish,
and pray to reign forever in my heart,
and, once you've crowned with fire the flowery altars,
then let the plans for celebration start.
Let wine speed nightfall, and from bowls of onyx
the scent of saffron make the whole room sweet;
the pipes be hoarse at midnight for our dancing,
and all our wit be broad as it is neat.
O let us feast with never a thought of slumber,
and deafen all the neighbors with our joy,
and dice to find out who among us shivers
under the lashing of the winged boy.
And when we've drunk a new day into being,
when Venus and the night their rites prepare,
sweet, come to bed: we'll celebrate together
the ritual that you were born to share.

III. xi

QUID MIRARE, MEAM SI VERSAT FEMINA VITAM . . .

Why do you marvel that she is the magnet
to which my life and I are wholly bound?
Why do you mock me as both slave and coward,
too weak to burst the chains that bind me round?
The seasoned sailor can foretell the tempest;
from his own wounds the soldier learns to fear.
Callow as you are now, I boasted like you.
Caution's hardwon—come learn of caution here.
With an unyielding yoke the bulls were conquered,
the seeds of battle sown upon the field,
the guardian snake's jaws closed—all by Medea
so that the fleece to Jason be revealed.
Penthesilea dared to join the Trojans
against the Greeks—that Amazonian queen
slain by Achilles, who in turn was vanquished
by her bright loveliness, too lately seen.
Omphale bathed in Lydian lakes, a beauty
so irresistible that Hercules,
whose columns propped the sky above a calmed world,
turned wheel, spun wool, with hands ill-made for these.
Semiramis established Persia's city,[50]
a solid mass within a great brick wall
through which two chariots might pass each other
and neither touch the other one at all;
she led the great Euphrates through the center
of Babylon, and made the Bactrians slaves.
Why should I list the sins of gods and heroes?
Jove makes us blush to see how he behaves.
Why should I tell of her who mocked our armies,[51]
took her own slaves as bedfellows, dared claim
the walls of Rome as fee from her foul lover,

and left the Senate trembling at her name?
O Alexandria, betrayal's birthplace,
O Memphis, bloodstained always with our woe,
where the sands stole from Pompey his three triumphs![52]
No other shame has brought Rome's pride so low.
Better for Pompey had he died at Naples,
or bowed his neck to Caesar as his son.
Ptolemy's queen,[53] that whore, that Macedonian,
whose dogfaced god fought Jove and nearly won—
think of her, how the Nile threatened the Tiber,
how Isis' rattles deafened all of Rome,
how that royal barge pursued the light-oared galley,
how on the Tarpeian Rock she made her home
and gave her edicts under Marius' statue!
Think of this city, Rome the seven-hilled,
shivering at the whims of such a woman,
fearing her threats, following where she willed!
Did this race break the axes of that Tarquin
whose arrogance has nicknamed him *The Proud*?
Shall we endure a woman-king? Let long life
be given Augustus—pray it, pray aloud!
Yet the gods drove her back at last to Egypt,
her hands were bound at last in Roman chains;
I saw those arms the sacred asps[54] had bitten,
I guessed the poison pouring through her veins.
"With such as Caesar, Rome need not have feared me,"
she said, in wine-engendered honesty.
Closing the gulf, Curtius was made immortal;
Decius on horseback broke the enemy.
Who does not know the bridge of brave Horatius,
or him who from the raven got his name?

The gods who made the walls of Rome will save them;
for us his Romans, Caesar does the same,
even from Jove's wrath. Where's the fleet of Scipio,
Camillus' standards, Pompey's Bosporus?
Where are the spoils of Hannibal, of Syphax,
of Pyrrhus, almost the victorious?
Apollo, tell how all of them were routed,
in one swift day of battle swept to death.
O sailor, coming home or weighing anchor,
honor Augustus' name with every breath!

III. xii

POSTUME, PLORANTEM POTUISTI LINQUERE GALLAM . . .

Postumus, could you leave your Galla weeping
and follow Caesar's standards into war?
What Parthian loot is worth her tears, her terror,
her certainty that you'll return no more?
If there is justice, may death take the venal
and him who loves arms more than Venus' gift!
Cold in your cloak, you'll drink of river water
out of a helmet you can scarcely lift;
and she, meanwhile, will pale at every rumor
for fear of what your courage may have cost—
lest foreign archer or gold-armored horseman
strike to the heart, and your dear life be lost;
lest she be sent an urn of your scant relics
(so those return whom death abroad may find).
Thrice blest to have a wife both chaste and faithful,
your blindness should have had another kind!—
one whom no fear for your welfare might harrow,
who'd let Rome's revels drive you from her mind.
Go without fear of that—Galla's not tempted;
only your cruelty will she forget.
If the gods send you home again in safety,
her kiss will show how much she loves you yet.
She'll be Penelope to your Ulysses
whose wanderings, like his, leave you no less—
he lived through ten years' war, survived the Thracians,
Gibraltar, the blind giant's[55] wrathfulness;
evaded Circe's guile, the lulling lotos,
Scylla, Charybdis, with their ebb and flow,
the bellowing oxen which the sun god's daughter
had pastured and the Greeks slew, to their woe;
He slipped from Circe's bed, for all her pleading;

he swam the deep how many nights and days?
he sought Tiresias in hell's deadly silence;
he heard the song the Sirens' voices raise,
and bent the bow to kill a hundred suitors,
victorious by the grace that Jove confers—
discovering his Penelope still faithful.
And Galla's loyalty is no less than hers.

III. xiii

QUAERITIS, UNDE AVIDIS NOX SIT PRETIOSA PUELLIS . . .

You ask why women's greed makes love so costly,
and why our strongboxes are Venus' loot.
Surely the answer's clear beyond all question—
the love of luxury is love's pursuit.
The ant brings gold dust, and the Indian steals it;[56]
in the Red Sea they dive for nautilus shells;
Tyre sends us, for a price, Tyrian purple;[57]
Araby, cinnamon—how rich it smells!
How can we guard our girls from such temptation—
even a woman like Penelope?
They flaunt themselves, decked out in spendthrifts' fortunes,
and wear their ill-got wealth for all to see.
They have no shame; there's nothing they won't ask for—
or if there is, they'll learn as they grow bold.
You know the Eastern law for a man's burial?
Before the next dawn rises, red and gold,
before the last torch lights the pyre he lies on,
his wives are struggling, with disheveled hair,
to be the first to join him where he's lying.
They count such sacrifice an honor there;
they give their breasts, their bodies, to the burning,
upon his ashes let their ashes lie.
What Roman bride would dare to be as faithful?
Rome's heroines are of an age gone by.
Envy with me the peaceful country couples
young long ago, and rich in fruit and grain.
They made their offerings of fresh-picked apples,
or blackberries, or lilies cool with rain,
mingled together in their woven baskets—
violets, or leaf-wrapped grapes; or tried to tame

a bright-winged bird, if they were quick to catch one,
whose colors put the rainbow's hues to shame.
It was by gifts like these they won the kisses
given them where the trees met overhead.
A deerskin made a coverlet for lovers,
and the soft grass for them was ample bed.
The branches of the pine gave grateful shadow;
to see a goddess naked was no sin.
The ram led back his ewes after their grazing
and at the wood god's door herded them in.
The gods and goddesses who loved the country
spoke at the altar only gentle words:
"Stranger, be welcome; in our paths unhindered
hunt, if you wish, our rabbits and our birds.
Whether you hunt with hounds or wade at fishing,
summon me down to be your comrade Pan."
But now these shrines lie empty and forgotten.
Piety's lost, and gold's the dream of man.
Gold's banished faith, and made of Roman justice
a mockery, a thing that's bought and sold.
Greed jeers at law, and, with the law corrupted,
chastity's gone as well, the pawn of gold.
Brennus, attacking Delphi, met hell fire there
when he defied Apollo's holy fane—
Parnassus, shaking, hurled upon his forces
thunder and lightning, rocks and snow and rain.
For gold alone the Thracian Polymestor
betrayed his Trojan ward, old Priam's son.
For a golden chain Eriphyla sent her husband
to fight a war he knew could not be won.[58]
Let me speak, Rome! You'll find me a true prophet.

Gold is your illness; you will die of gold.
I speak the truth, but no one will believe me,
as none believed Cassandra's words of old.
She cried aloud that Troy's doom would be Paris,
that the Greek horse brought in a treacherous freight.
O, had her king, her country, listened to her!
The tongue that none would hear foretold their fate.

III. xiv

MULTA TUAE, SPARTE, MIRAMUR IURA PALAESTRAE . . .

The Spartan wrestlers and their rules amaze me—
but, more, the school in which their women train,
where they may exercise their naked bodies
on the same ground on which those wrestlers strain,
and where the swift ball tricks the hand stretched for it
and the hooked rod guides the hoop's rolling flight.
That dusty figure at the goal's a woman;
a woman's in this rough-and-tumble fight!
Another binds her eager hands for boxing;
a fourth girl whirls the discus overhead,
or, with the hoarfrost on her hair, goes racing
after her father's hounds, where they have sped;
puts a horse through his paces, slings a sword on
her white thigh, or a helmet on her head,
fierce as the Amazonian warriors[59] bathing
barebreasted in Thermodon's river bed,
like Helen, when with Castor and with Pollux
she carried arms (so the report persists)
nor blushed before her brothers, one the horseman
and one the champion who fought with fists.
This is that Sparta that indulges lovers,
where couples hand-in-hand in public walk,

no girl goes guarded, no one rants of honor,
none dreads a husband's wrath or threatening talk.
All unannounced, there you may state your business
with neither deputy nor long delay;
a lover's not beguiled by nonessentials,
his dear does not arrange her hair all day.
But here where Cynthia walks are people, people—
I cannot even reach her through that crowd.
I don't know what to wear or how to hail her.
The path I tread what doubts and darkness shroud!

Rome, learn from Sparta's healthy point of view.
Yield! Give us further cause to honor you!

III. xv

SIC EGO NON ULLOS IAM NORIM IN AMORE TUMULTUS . . .

No storms henceforth, I beg you, in our loving,
nor any endless wakeful empty nights!
When I had passed beyond my boyhood shyness
and was permitted love and all its rights,
it was Lycinna brought me that first knowledge,
giving a heart that I could not repay.
Now, almost three years since then, I remember
scarcely ten words of all we had to say.
Your love has buried all; no other woman
has made of me her captive, to this day.

*   *   *

Dirce be witness—Dirce mad with terror
lest Lycus leave her for Antiope!
How often did the queen burn her fair tresses
or clutch her face in jealous agony—
how often pile new tasks on her handmaiden,
force her to sleep on the unyielding ground,
house her in filthy darkness, and refuse her
water for lips too parched to utter sound!
Jove, will you so desert your once-beloved?
See how the chains have rubbed her white hands raw!
Can you, a god, allow such degradation?
Where's justice for her, save in Jove's own law?
Yet by her own strength, and with no one helping,
those same galled hands have broken through their chain,
and, running, trembling, she has climbed Cithaeron
to hide there, shivering in the icy rain.
She heard the river water rushing past her
and shuddered lest that sound be Dirce's feet.
The sons she'd borne to Jove were undecided,
hedged, would not help their mother in defeat—

till, like the waves that slowly cease their tumult
once the wind slackens over storm-swept seas
and the shores echo less and less the waters,
calm with despair she sank upon her knees.
Then her sons' guardian would have cheered his charges—
they saved their mother, and they put to rout
Dirce, bound to a bull, her body broken.
Here is Jove's justice now, and who can doubt?
Antiope, you may boast of Dirce's dying
that hideous death; the fields of Zethus reek
with blood; your other son Amphion, singing
of victory, stands on Cithaeron's peak.
Cynthia, torment any but Lycinna.
Jealousy knows no limits; put it by.
You've heard our story, hers and mine; it's ended.
You are my love, and shall be till I die.

III. xvi

NOX MEDIA, ET DOMINAE MIHI VENIT EPISTULA NOSTRAE . . .

At midnight came a message from my mistress
bidding me come to Tivoli in all haste,
where the white hills heave upward like huge towers
and spreading pools with Anio's foam are laced.
What should I do? entrust myself to darkness
where any hand might stab me in the back?
Yet if my fear should conquer my obedience,
her tears, her rage, would put me on the rack.
I had sinned once and done a whole year's penance—
for me there's never mercy in her heart.
I tell myself, but who would harm a lover?
Lovers are proof against the deadliest art;
unarmed, unscathed, they move through barbarous country;
though they meet savages, they find no foes.
The moon, the stars, make bright the paths they wander,
and as their guide, Love, the torchbearer, goes;
the surly watchdog sees them and is silent—
for them the road is safe at any hour.
Who'd have a lover's blood on hands or conscience?
Venus herself protects us with her power.
And were I killed, my body would be buried
with every ceremony, every rite;
she would bring offerings to my grave, and flowers,
would come to watch beside it day and night.
Let her not have me lie, though, where the crowds pass,
where men's footsteps would pound above my head.
So many lovers' tombs are thus dishonored!
May tall trees shade the place where I lie dead,
or may the desert hide me—but in pity,
do not condemn my ghost to haunt the city!

III. xvii

NUNC, O BACCHE, TUIS HUMILES ADVOLVIMUR ARIS . . .

Your altars, Bacchus, see a suppliant kneeling—
O father, give me peace, prosper my sails!
You help me suffer Venus and her tantrums.
Wine as a cure for sorrow never fails.
You can bring lovers close or you can part them—
O Bacchus, wash this weakness from my soul!
You have your love;[60] you brought her, lynx-drawn, skyward,
in whose life Theseus played a sorry role.
But love, for me, is only fire and torment,
a sickness you or death alone may heal.
Night can be hell itself for lonely lovers
unless you ease the hope and fear they feel.
Leave my wits reeling and my step uncertain,
if you will give as well your gift of sleep.
I'll pay you homage, I will plant you vineyards
no beast will dare come near, such watch I'll keep.
I'll tend your vats, the red juice overflowing,
my feet stained purple as I tread the press—
if you, the horned god,[61] give my life its life-blood,
then I shall praise aloud your godliness.
I'll tell how you were born of one Jove blasted,[62]
how Indian warriors fled from Nysa's bands,[63]
how you drove mad the impious king Lycurgus,
and Pentheus, murdered by the Maenads' hands;
and how those Tuscan sailors, turned to dolphins,[64]
leaped from a ship whose mast was all a vine,
and how for you the brooks ran sweet in Naxos
so people stooped and drank from them your wine.
Your white neck bowed under the wreaths of ivy,
you'll wear a Lydian turban on your hair;
the scented oil will leave your smooth skin shining,

your flowing robes be white, your feet be bare.
And Thebes, to honor you, shall sound the timbrels;
goat-footed Pan play on his pipes of reed;
the dancers follow where, with her turret-headdress,
Cybele and the clanging cymbals lead.
At the temple gate the priest with a golden ladle
shall dip from the sacred bowl the holy wine—
and I'll sing your virtues not as a poetaster
but borrowing Pindar's voice to make it mine.

O Bacchus, in return, grant me release:
free me from her, great god! O give me peace!

III. xviii

CLAUSUS AB UMBROSO QUA ALLUDIT PONTUS AVERNO . . .

Where the sea laughs, cut off from dark Avernus,
and beats on Baia's pools with every wave,
where Hercules' road[65] echoes to the sea pulse,
where the Trumpeter of Troy[66] lies in his grave,
where cymbals clashed, exalting Dionysus
who came to bless the towns that men have built—
what baleful god stands now at Baia's waters,
darkened with guilt?
Here, in this town, Marcellus died. From Baia
his spirit wanders on the Stygian shore.
His mother's grace, his goodness, could not save him;
Caesars, lords of the world, could do no more.
No use to him the theater bright with awnings
and all its throng; no use his mother's care.
Less than a score of years—but O what glory
was compassed there!
Go, move in pride; go dreaming of your triumphs,
of you the hero all men rise to cheer;
you with your cloth of gold, in games gem-studded—
the fires of death take all that men hold dear.
To death at last we come, the base, the noble.
This is the road that every man must tread,
placating Cerberus, boarding the skiff of Charon
who herds the dead.
Would you save yourself with walls of brass and iron?
From even that shelter death will drag you out.
Mighty Achilles, handsome Nereus, Croesus—
valor and beauty and wealth: all put to rout.
But we consign to Charon only the body.
The inward essential spirit—that will go
starward along the way triumphant Claudius
and Caesar know.

148

III. xix

OBICITUR TOTIENS A TE MIHI NOSTRA LIBIDO . . .

How often you taunt me: *Only man is lustful!*
You lie. For women, lust is lord no less.
Once (and how soon!) they learn to mock the modest,
there is no limit to their wantonness.
Sooner a fire die down that feeds on dry grass,
sooner a stream run backward to the source,
marshes and quicksand offer men safe harbor,
cliffs welcome back the sailor from his course—
more chance of these than that a man may check you,
clutching and writhing, panting and possessed.
Think of Pasiphae, yielding to the proud bull,
her head in heifer horns of fir wood dressed;
of Tyro, ready for Eripeus' taking
but yielding to the sea god in disguise;
of Myrrha, incestuous daughter turned to myrtle,
her act a scandal even to women's eyes.
Or stern half-mad Medea, sacrificing
her children to a passion beyond shame;
and Clytemnestra, that whore of Mycenae
shaming the house of Pelops with her name;
and Scylla, clipping the lock of hair, betraying
her father and her fatherland to Crete
for love of Minos—such was Scylla's dowry
who opened Nisus' portals to defeat.
(A happier flame for other wedding torches!)
Bound to the Cretan rudder, so they tell,
Scylla has drowned, and Minos, man of justice,
moved to his rightful place as judge of hell.

III. xx

CREDIS EUM IAM POSSE TUAE MEMINISSE FIGURAE . . .

Can you believe he'll have a thought to spare you,
who sails away, content to leave your bed?
Is this a lover, gone to seek a fortune,
greedy for gain, blind to the tears you shed?
Only a fool would give his oath such credence;
twenty to one, he's found a new love now.
Not I. You have all graces, every beauty;
you wear ancestral laurels on your brow.
No house needs wealth that has a faithful lover,
as I am faithful. Darling, come to bed—
this is our night. O moon and sun, give over!
Moon, while we lie here, linger overhead.
And sun, your welcome long outworn, take pity:
shorten your course, put down your stubborn light.
But first are oaths to take for this my new love,
a pact for us to make, a pledge to write;
and Love himself will set his seal upon it,
and Ariadne sign our testament.
Venus shall rouse us into loving warfare
from easy hours in conversation spent—
love's bed must be protected by love's promise,
or no just gods avenge love's sleepless guard
and lust will break the fetters set upon it—
if our vows hold us, love may live unmarred.
Whoever breaks those vows made at the altars,
whoever's faithless to the given word—
may all the griefs of love fasten upon him;
from every gossip's lips his name be heard;
at the shut window, desperation seize him.
And let him love, but let no loving ease him.

III. xxi

MAGNUM ITER AD DOCTAS PROFICISCI COGAR ATHENAS . . .

I must set forth to Athens, home of wisdom—
Athens may free me from my servitude.
The sight of Cynthia only feeds my passion;
how long would love survive without that food?
I am no willing captive—I'd escape him
could men escape the watch that Eros keeps;
for she refuses me, will see me rarely,
lies on my bed's edge fully clothed, and sleeps.
There's no help for it. Love, leave my heart empty,
empty as eyes that look at her no more.
Men, on our way; let's send our vessel seaward;
draw lots to see which pair first takes an oar.
The gods are kind. Run the sails up the lanyards;
let the breeze move us through the ocean swell.
O towers of Rome and all the friends I leave there,
farewell—and love, for better or worse, farewell.

And now across the unknown Adriatic,
trusting the sea gods, I must make my way
through the Ionian Sea, and, once at Corinth,
anchor within that quiet-watered bay;
then, for the rest, must walk across the Isthmus[67]
whose fields hold back the sea on either side,
and, where the port of Athens gives me welcome,
climb cityward, the Thesean road[68] for guide.
The Academia will cleanse my spirit;
you, Epicurus, you will clear my mind.
Demosthenes, make eloquent my speeches!
What wit, Menander, in your works I'll find—
what sustenance, what joy, in famous paintings
and statues formed from ivory or bronze!

Time or the severing sea must heal the sorrow
hidden so long, must break at last these bonds—
and I shall die because the gods have spoken,
with honor; not as one whom love has broken.

III. xxii

FRIGIDA TAM MULTOS PLACUIT TIBI CYZICUS ANNOS . . .

Tullus, you stay too long there on the Black Sea
where northern waters wash the narrow strand,
where, they say, Pluto vanished with his captive,
where ivory statues of Cybele stand.
I know you love those far cities of Helle—
and yet I call you back from that bleak land.
Splendid to see the heavens on Atlas' shoulders,
the Gorgon's head severed by Perseus' hand,

Geryon's oxen; the dust where Antaeus wrestled
with Hercules, or the nymph dance of the West;
splendid to churn the waters of the Phasis
through which the pine wood Argo once progressed—
timber from Pelion, shaped to make the vessel
that with the dove's help met the rocks' cruel test[69]—
splendid to visit Delos, Asia Minor,
the seven-channelled river,[70] and the rest—

yet Rome has marvels greater than all the others;
nature herself has made our city great.
This is a place of peace and not of bloodshed;
honor and fame were granted us by fate.
We've made our stand through faith no less than fighting;
even our wrath we learn to mitigate.
The Anio, the Umbrian Clitumnus,
the Marcian conduit[71]—these we celebrate.

Here's Alba's lake, and leaf-reflecting Nemi;[72]
here Pollux' horse drank at the healing spring;
here no horned snakes slide by on slimy bellies;
not of sea monsters do our sailors sing.
Here is no chained and innocent Andromeda,
no sun god shocked by Atreus' banqueting,[73]

no log that meant the death of Meleager,
waiting the torch his mother herself would bring.

Here is no Pentheus torn by the Bacchantes.
No girl need die so that a fleet may sail.[74]
June would change no maiden to a heifer[75]
with tawny coat and hoofs and horns and tail.
Sinis would not break men on trees, and no ships,
lured by false beacons, try to land, and fail.[76]
This is your country, Tullus. You were born here;
seek here the honors that no years can stale.

Rome's life, Rome's future—these are your concern;
and here the girl you love waits your return.

III. xxiii

ERGO TAM DOCTAE NOBIS PERIERE TABELLAE . . .

All my filled notebooks lost, and vanished with them
so much good writing—where could have have gone?
I've used them for so long now they've grown dingy;
no need for any seal set thereupon.
Rough drafts of notes, they kept love close in absence,
and kept me, absent, vivid to her eyes.
Plain things they were, no golden trimmings on them;
the wax was thin, the frame of no great size.
To any casual glance they'd have no value,
and yet they won for me some small success.
Sometimes she'd write to me on them: *I'm angry.*
What's your excuse for last night's tardiness?
You thought you'd find a prettier girl than this one?
You've spread more rumors that will do me wrong?
or, on a happier note: *Come soon, my darling,*
where love will make you welcome all night long.
Words from my lively chattering quick-witted Cynthia,
offering us long hours for love to fill—
and now some merchant tucks them in his ledger
or, on the back, scribbles his greasy bill!
There's a reward in gold for their returning—
who'd keep the trash when he could claim the prize?
Print the address—the Esquiline—down here, boy,
and post the notice to catch all men's eyes.

III. xxiv

FALSA EST ISTA TUAE, MULIER, FIDUCIA FORMAE . . .

O Cynthia, your beauty may betray you!
It was my praise that made you overproud.
You'll never have another judge as partial—
but now I wish my praise had been less loud.
You and your loveliness were all my poems—
love closed my eyes to what you really are:
tricked by your art, mistaking it for nature,
I called you fairer than the evening star.
My father's friends have tried in vain to cure me;
no incantation taught me disbelief,
and, driven by neither fire nor knife, but shipwrecked
on desperate seas, I cried aloud my grief.
Venus has burned me, captive in her cauldron,
my twisted hands behind my back tied fast—
but like a fleet come safe through shifting currents
now I'm in harbor, and my anchor cast.
Winds' tumult and tides' roar—I can forget them;
I waken calm to find my wounds all healed.
At Moderation's altar let me worship!
Jove would not heed my prayers; his ears were sealed.

III. xxv

RISUS ERAM POSITIS INTER CONVIVIA MENSIS . . .

Loud jeering greeted my name at the banquet table;
the dirtiest mind would smear me with its dirt.
For five long years I've been your slave, and faithful—
but, now I'm free, you are the one who's hurt.
Tears are no use; I fell into that trap once.
You weep to trick me, but I've grown alert.

Not that I shall not weep myself, but briefly;
my wrongs, your yoke, are things I can't forget.
Farewell, O door still echoing to my pleading,
door I could not break down, stubbornly set!
As for you, Cynthia, let age creep on you;
let each new wrinkle mark a new regret.

Count every white hair; pull them out each morning
before the glass that mocks your fading face;
and know, like me, that you are barred from heaven,
and see a young usurper in your place!
Cry out, poor shrunken hag, for my forgiveness.
Beauty, once damned, can offer you no grace.

BOOK FOUR

IV. i

HOC QUODCUMQUE VIDES, HOSPES, QUA MAXIMA ROMA EST . . . .

Stranger, where great Rome stands were grass and hillocks
before the harbor welcomed the Trojan prows,
and on the hill now sacred to Apollo
Evander's exiled cattle used to browse.
From gods of clay have come our golden temples—
on crude shrines first the gods their grace conferred.
The old kings thundered from a rocky pulpit.
The Tiber's taste was strange to the Trojan herd.
Atop the Palatine, the house of Remus
marks what once seemed to him a mighty realm.
Our fathers, wolfskin-clad, met in their council
where now the toga'd statesmen hold the helm.
A hundred men might gather in a meadow—
their Senate, summoned by a trumpet there.
No rippled awnings shaded theater-goers
nor let the scent of saffron fill the air.
Men sought no foreign gods; the people trembled
before the ritual their fathers taught—
purified by the straw-heaps burned to Pales,
as now the horse's blood to Mars is brought.
To honor Vesta, thin-flanked cows paraded,
and donkeys, garlanded with loaves of bread.

The shepherd piped and offered a sheep's entrails;
the crossroad altars reeked where the fat pig bled.
At the Lupercalia, men in goatskin aprons
ran scourging all to make a fruitful land.
Not blazing in fearful armor, but barebreasted
they went to fight, a burnt-hard stake in the hand.
Tatius' wealth was flocks, and his kinsman Lycmon
wore a wolfskin helmet in his warlike deeds.
Thence the tribes—Luceres, Ramnes, Titienses;
and thence, too, Romulus, driving the four white steeds.
Bovillae, Rome's suburb now, seemed a city in those days,
and Gabii, that's shrunk to a ghost town now.
When Rome was remote from Fidenae, the metropolis
was Ascanius' Alba, built where he found the sow.[77]
The Roman today shares only his name with his fathers;
he does not believe that the she-wolf suckled the boys.
O Trojans, you came in search of happier fortunes;
to our shore sailed what was left of that fleet of Troy's,
led by the gods who rescued old Anchises
and his son from the burning wrath of the wooden horse.
Out of that race came Brutus and the Decii
and Caesar, set by Venus on his course
toward greatness, with the arms of Troy resurgent.
Here there were fanes that Iulus' gods could fill,
once the dark Sibyl, trembling over the tripod,
called Remus to proclaim the holy hill.[78]
We know the truths that mad Cassandra chanted—
prophet disdained; true prophet, all the same:
Turn back, O Greeks! Your victory is worthless!
With Jove's help, a new Troy shall gain new fame!
O wolf of Mars, what better nurse for our country!
out of your sustenance what walls have sprung!
To do them honor calls for a voice far stronger
than that in which my minor notes are sung.

Yet out of this heart my song, however slender,
offers my country all its humble praise.
Ennius, crown my work with wildflower garlands,
and Bacchus, let your ivy deck my days!
May they boast of my books where I was born, in Umbria,
as they boast of Callimachus and his widespread fame.
Let those who come to Assisi, there in the valley,
reckon its glory by my verse, my name.
Smile on me, Rome, sovereign and subject! Romans,
wish me a sign: bird song at my right hand.
Listen: *Troy fell that Trojan Rome might follow*—
so starts my tale of what has made our land,
its history, its holy rites, its perils.
Pegasus, forward now, to my command!

IV. i a

QUO RUIS IMPRUDENS, VAGE, DICERE FATA, PROPERTI . . .

Propertius, what folly gives you these grandiose visions?
the thread of your verse is far too thin for these.
It will not work, for you've lost Apollo's blessing;
you'll turn to discords your fragile melodies.
I'll give you the truth, if I have any power
to read the stars and interpret their every sign.
I am Babylonian, and my name is Horos,
son of Orops. Conon's an ancestor of mine.
I am no less than they, as my gods are witness.
My books deceive no man; they mean what they say.
There are charlatans who turn their power to profit,
trick Jove with gold, decipher the heavens for pay—
the stars of Jupiter and of Mars the greedy,
of Saturn, that sign of universal grief;
the star of the fish and the terrible star of the lion,
and Capricorn, high over a western reef.
It was I who warned Arria, when she bore her twin sons
(she trained them as soldiers, though the gods forbade),
they would never bring their spears to their father's altar—
and now in a double tomb the two are laid:
Lupercus the horseman, his slashed face bleeding, his steed gone,
defended himself, half-blinded, before he fell,
and dying Gallus, whose charge was the eagle standard,
bloodied the ground and the carved bird beaks as well.
Poor boys, their death foredoomed by their wilful mother!—
but it gave me only grief to be proven right.
And I was the one, when Cynara struggled in childbed
and Juno prolonged the labor with all her might—
I cried, *Make Juno a vow she cannot be deaf to!*
She did as I said, and Juno allowed the birth.
Such truths are not found in the caves of Jupiter Ammon,

nor in entrails burned to show the gods' will on earth.
No seer is my equal if he trusts to the crow's flight
or the magic waters that hold the souls of the dead.
No. The way to the truth lies along the path of the heavens,
the five zones of the sky far overhead.
Ask Calchas, who gave the word for embarkation
when the ships, unwilling, left Aulis' rocky bay.
Ask Calchas, who thrust the sword at Iphigenia
that Agamemnon might go on his fatal way
and the Greeks find death! O Trojans, disheartened and weeping,
never despair. You will end the long pursuit;
Nauplius puts the torch to the treacherous beacons
and the whole Greek fleet is lost with its Trojan loot.
Drunken Ajax rapes the holy priestess[79]
though Minerva forbids him even to come near.
So much for history. By my own method
I'll chart your past and future for you to hear.
You were born to wealth and pride in ancient Umbria,
(so far am I right? what errors do I make?)
the town, Mevania; cool hills and hollows;
mist-bound on summer days, the Umbrian lake;
Assisi's walls, forever climbing upward—
the walls all men will know who read your verse.
When you were young—too young—you lost your father,
and every day you fared a little worse:
the great house and the fields, the stabled oxen,
seized and allotted soldiers of the state.
You offered up the locket of your childhood
to your mother's gods, you put on man's estate,
foreswore the lawcourts and the Forum's tumult,
and set yourself to see if you could write.
Elegy is your field, a difficult business;
let your success inspire the neophyte.
Exalt the wars of Venus as you suffer

her wounds, your heart the pawn of Cupid's will.
Often and often in those wars a winner,
you'll find one girl who will escape you still.
Hooked fish, you'll shake free of the hook, or think so—
only to find the rod and barb still hold.
Her whim shall rule your coming and your going;
you will not even weep unless you're told.
She'll be untrue. Guard her door, seal it—useless:
some chink, some crack, will let the sweet cheat go.
I warn you: travel, tossed by gales and whirlwinds,
or walk unarmed among an armored foe,
or feel the earth quake—she's a greater danger,
this greedy child of the Crab,[80] your world, your woe.

IV. ii

QUID MIRARE MEAS TOT IN UNO CORPORE FORMAS . . .

Is it so strange to find the body Protean?
I, the god Vertumnus, change my form at will.
Long since, without regret, I left my homeland
when the wars came. Though I'm a Tuscan, still
I need these crowds more than an ivory temple;
the Forum makes a tumult in my blood.
Old Tiber has not always kept this channel—
there were great marshes that it used to flood;
and when it yielded men that land for plowing,
I am the god they named to mark the change.
To me are given the fruits of the year's harvest:
all orbits and cycles come within my range:
translucent grapes, grown dark in a rounded cluster,
corn with its milky kernels swelling the ear,
great ripening cherries with their sheen of purple,
summer's mulberries, plums at the turn of the year.
The farmer worships me with wreaths and garlands,
grafting an apple on the pear tree's stock.
Believe the god's own story: there's further warrant
for my name, a truth that liars and fools may mock—
I can change my form with my nature and still delight you;
whatever you wish me to turn into, I can.
Dress me in silks, I'll have all of a young girl's beauty;
see me in a toga and swear that I'm a man.
Or put a twist of hay around my forehead—
now I'm the farmer whose sickle cuts the grass.
I've been in wars and won praise as a soldier.
I glean the meadows after the reapers pass.
I am sober within the law courts, but at a banquet
you would guess that the wine had gone to my rose-crowned head.
It takes no more than a turban to make Bacchus,

and only a lyre to make me Apollo instead.
A net slung over my shoulder, I'll hunt; as a fowler,
be the god who helps him snare the bird with his reed.
I can be a charioteer, or, acrobatic,
leap from one horse to another at top speed.
All I need is a rod to become a fisherman;
in a ragged robe I can peddle spruce, if I must.
I can stoop like a shepherd over a crook, or bring you
a basket of roses through the heat and dust.
The best of every species in the garden
is given to me, as farmers have always known—
cucumbers, striped dark-green; gourds with round bellies;
rush-tied cabbages—these are all my own.
Even the humblest field flower must be added
to the garland-offering set upon my head.
What other name than mine for one so changeful?—
disguised anew, the old mask hardly shed.
Rome, you had reason to reward my Tuscans
(isn't Tuscany the name of a modern street?)
when, after the Sabine wars, one Roman faction
attacked another and brought it to defeat.
I saw the breaking ranks and the broken weapons;
I watched the enemy turn his back and flee.
O Jupiter, let the white-robed throng of Romans
move past my statue, and let them worship me.

My story has six lines more, but I would not keep you
from your court of law to hear the end thereof . . .
Once I was carved from a rough-cut chunk of maple;
I was never a wealthy god, in the city I love,

until Mamurius cast my form in metal
(may the earth rest lightly on hands that had such skill!)
and made the intractable bronze obey his genius.
His single work—may it win new honor still!

IV. iii

HAEC ARETHUSA SUO MITTIT MANDATA LYCOTAE . . .

I am your Arethusa, you my Lycotas,
and this is my message, if, absent, you still are mine.
I send you this letter, illegible and blotted
and blurred with tearstains defacing every line—
if you cannot read it at all, so faint the writing,
know that death's own hand is upon my hand.
The world is your province; twice you've gone to Persia,
told of the armored heroes of that far land,
seen Scythia and the Britons' painted chariots,
and over wave-washed sunburned India passed.
Is this a marriage? is the night forgotten
when I, a stranger to love, yielded at last?
Surely the wedding torch they held before me
burned balefully as a torch that lights the dead;
hell's water sprinkled me; the god was absent;
they set the wreath askew upon my head.
On every wind I post prayers for your safety—
for the fourth time I weave you a soldier's cloak.
Perish the man who made of bones a trumpet,
a rampart from some unoffending oak!
He and not Ocnus should be set to twisting
the endless straw rope that the donkey ate.
O tell me—does the breastplate rub your arms raw?
the spear chafe hands not meant for such a weight?
Yet I would rather these should make you suffer
than have a girl's teeth scar your neck and lip.
They say you're haggard. Is it me you long for?
will your pallor go when you board a home-bound ship?
And as for me, when the night I hate approaches,
I kiss the weapons that you did not take,
I toss till the coverlet is a mass of wrinkles,

I wait for the birds that sing the dawn to wake.
All the long winter nights I spend in weaving
so that you will not lack warm clothes to wear;
I sew that cloth, so brave a Tyrian purple,
wondering, *Will a sword pierce here, or there?*
I learn what rivers flow across Armenia,
how far, unwatered, a Parthian horse will go.
I have a painted map of the world to study,
and I search for the places you have come to know:
lands that are clammy with cold or baked in sunlight.
To bring you home, I can tell what wind must blow.
My sister sympathizes; my nurse, poor woman,
insists that the winter holds you landlocked there.
I envy bare-breasted Hippolyte, holding the long spear,
tucking under a helmet her long soft hair.
If the Roman camps would open their gates to women,
I would follow you faithfully in any war—
even to Scythia's mountains, where Jove in winter
freezes the rivers over, shore to shore.
All love is great, but the greatest love is in marriage:
Venus herself sees that it grows no less.
I cannot walk proudly if you are not here to admire.
What's a crystal ring, or purple silk for a dress?
All things are deaf; when I listen, I hear the silence;
only once a month we open the house-gods' shrine.
Your puppy Craugis comes to lie beside me
where you should lie, and comforts me with her whine.
I cover the altars with flowers; I wreathe the crossroads
with branches; I set the incense out to burn.
If an owl moans from a tree, or the lamp flame sputters
and I pour wine on it, to make sure your return—

that day we sacrifice the lambs of this springtime,
and the priests in their robes beg favors of the gods.
O my husband, do not strain too hard for glory
or fight for loot against unfavoring odds
when the stones of the twisted slings are flying around you
or the Parthian horseman aims his deadly bow!
But—till the war's over and you ride in triumph
with the headless spear of honor—till this is so,
remember the oath we made at the marriage altar.
If you break that oath, you will break my hold on life.
At the gate of the Appian Way I shall offer your armor
to the gods if they bring you safely back to your wife.

IV. iv

TARPEIUM NEMUS ET TARPEIAE TURPE SEPULCRUM . . .

I'll tell you now of the shameful tomb of Tarpeia,
the Tarpeian rock, the capture of holy ground.
This was the hill that Tatius, king of the Sabines,
ringed with a maple stockade, and the camp with a mound.
Can you imagine Rome when the Sabine trumpet
echoed among the rocks where Jove held sway?—
when Sabine javelins stood in the Roman Forum
from which come laws that rule the world today?
Rome was a town with only her hills for protection:
where our Senate stands, the war horse drank from a spring;
there were pleasant groves, and glens of rock and ivy,
and small tree-shadowed brooks made a murmuring.
Thick leaves sheltered the shepherd; you'd hear him piping
his sheep to the brook when the sun was overhead.
Tarpeia would offer spring water to the goddess
out of an earthenware urn that bowed her head.
Even a thousand deaths would not be sufficient
to punish a girl who betrayed the sacred fire.
She watched Rome's enemy Tatius ride on the flatlands,
his helm high-plumed, his spear flashing even higher,
and the earthen jar slipped from her trembling fingers
as she worshipped his handsome face and his royal attire.
She would say she must wash her hair in running water;
complain that the innocent moon had an evil charm;
bring to the nymphs great sheaves of lilies, praying
that no Roman spear might ever do Tatius harm.
She would climb the Capitoline in the cloudy morning,
heedless of thorny branches that scratched and tore,
and there where unforgiving Jove might hear her,
she grieved aloud for the deeper wounds she bore—
"Fires and tents that mark the camp of Tatius,

Sabine armor, beautiful shield and sword,
I would sit as a slave at the Sabine household altars
if a glimpse of that godlike face were my reward.
Vesta, my sin must mean your desecration.
Farewell then, Rome, and the seven hills of Rome!
That horse whose mane I have watched him smooth so often
shall bear me to him; his camp shall be my home.
What difference whether Scylla's waist is girdled
with hideous dogs to punish the parricide?
or if Ariadne betrays the bull to Theseus
at the Cretan palace, threading the maze inside?
It will shame all Roman women if the handmaid
give over the goddess—I know this past all doubt.
If you find no flame before Minerva's altar
in the temple, my guilty tears have put it out.
Tomorrow, they say, are the rites of purification:
Tatius, come to the ridge of this thorny hill—
but watch your footing; the pathway can betray you,
slippery when the hidden waters spill.
O if only I had the Muses' magic,
then I would know the words to help my love!
You should be wearing royal robes, all embroidered,
not that rough wolfskin your tunic is fashioned of.
Shall I reign beside you? shall I bear your children
in your Sabine halls? My dowry is all Rome.
Marry—or if you will, take me in vengeance
for the Sabine women stolen from their home.
I can come between the forces in their fighting—
as Tatius' bride, atone for the Roman theft.
Let the wedding trumpet drown the noise of battle;
on our marriage bed be all the war that is left.

Listen—the bugle sounds; it is almost morning.
The stars slip into the ocean, far to the west.
I pray I shall dream of you; no other vision
could give me courage while I try to rest,"
Her voice trailed out in sleep; she put her head down,
not knowing that wilder furies made her their prey,
for Vesta sent fires to rage in her very marrow,
and in vengeance drove her servant to obey—
until, like an Amazon, her clothing tattered,
she ran with her hair blown wild and her breasts all bare.

The feast day dawned—Parilia, they called it,
marking the first walls built by the Romans there:
a shepherds' festival spread through the city,
with stalls and tables heaped with country food;
the crowd goes jumping, drunk and dusty-footed,
over piles of burning straw on the roadway strewed.
Romulus ordered a holiday for the watchmen,
truce from the fight, for the camp a day of rest.
Tarpeia chose the place and the hour of meeting—
she made the pact; no other Roman guessed.
On the mudslick path, for once unguarded, Tatius
cut down the dogs before they began to bark.
But Jupiter looks down on the sleeping city,
planning Tarpeia's punishment in the dark—
what is fit for her who has opened the gate to the Sabines,
betrayed her people, named the day she would wed?
Tatius will punish her—she is only worth despising.
Marry, he says, *and here is your marriage bed!*
At the word, his comrades crush her under their piled shields—
a dowry due to such dishonor and shame.
The rock and the hill have taken their name from Tarpeia
but she does not deserve that we should remember that name.

IV. v

TERRA TUUM SPINIS OBDUCAT, LENA, SEPULCRUM . . .[81]

May thorns and briers cover the earth you lie in,
and the thirst you hated torture your ghost in hell!
May your wandering spirit search in vain for quiet
and shudder when Cerberus' howls of hunger swell!
She is the worst of the omens lovers meet with;
her evil could have seduced Hippolytus,
or forced Penelope, forgetting Ulysses,
to take to her bed the braggart Antinous.
Against her will the steel cannot reach the magnet;
she can make a bird stepmother to the nest.
The herbs she gathers and puts in that trench of magic
will turn a stone to water at her behest.
She can put a spell on the moon to do her bidding,
or come as a prowling wolf when the night wind wails,
or, by her slyness, blind a jealous husband,
or tear out the eyes of a crow with her fingernails.
With the owls she plots my death, and makes a potion
from the slimy discharge that comes from a mare in heat.
How smooth was her tongue as she turned her sorcery on you,
intent as a mole no stony path can defeat!
"If you dream of the golden shores of the Dorozantes,"
she would say, "or the dye from a Tyrian shell instead,
or silk from the land of Eurypylus, son of Hercules,
or crumbling figures cut from a golden bed,
or porcelain goblets fired in a kiln of Parthia,
or the treasures with which palm-shaded Thebes is crammed—
why, down with the gods! Break oaths, let lies take over!
The chaste are cheated. Chastity be damned!
Say that you have a husband: your value's doubled.
Be chary; love is whetted by abstinence.
If he rages and tears his hair, it is all to your profit—

you can name your price when your injured pride relents.
Then, when he's bought you back and you've set the hour,
say the rites of Isis forbid lovemaking today.
Let your slave remind him that gifts are pleasant in April
and that your birthday falls on the Ides of May.
He is your puppet. Go to your desk and scribble:
if he trembles with jealous suspicion, he's lost all pride;
let him see on your throat fresh marks that he will be certain
were made by the teeth of some rival, while he was denied—
but never delight, as Medea did, in nagging;
she dared to beg for love, and was cast aside.
Take as your model Thais, the famous actress
in Menander's plays, though her price was a little higher.
With each lover change your approach. If he brags of his singing,
join in a drunken duet while you strum on the lyre.
Tell your gatekeeper, 'Watch; have they gifts? If they're
     empty-handed,
don't bother to wake from your sleep by the barred door.'
Take any sailor so long as he has the money,
or any hulking soldier back from the war,
or even some barbarian bought in the slave mart
where with whitened feet he has danced to show he is strong.
It's the money that counts and not the hand that gives it.
Poetry pays no bills, once you've heard the song.
Dear love, dear life,[82] *you do not need adorning—*
hair curled, silk rustling down your slender side . . . !
If he cannot bring that silk as a gift, then silence.
Let his verses die unheard, as they should have died.
While your face is smooth, while your blood is rich with its
     springtime,
use the nights well, for time gives beauty short shrift.

I have seen the hot wind scorch the roses of Paestum
before their heads had had a chance to lift."

Acanthis gave her advice. I could only suffer
until you could count the bones beneath my skin.
But now, O Venus, a dove for my thank-offering:
the tables are turned; my luck is coming in.
I saw that wrinkled throat wracked by her coughing,
I saw the bloodstained spittle stain her teeth,
I saw her dying of plague in a shed's rough shelter
with her father's blanket for her to shiver beneath.
For funeral pomp, a borrowed band on her thin hair,
a headdress faded and filthy, and nothing more—
for mourner, only the dog that growled so often
when I would try to slip the bolts on your door.
Acanthis, I give you a broken-necked wine jar for tombstone;
may a wild fig tree take root and grow from your bones,
and if any who love pass by, may they curse your witchcraft
and batter this grave of yours with jagged stones!

IV. vi

SACRA FACIT VATES; SINT ORA FAVENTIA SACRIS . . .

The sacrifice is ready. Be still, that it prosper.
At my altar hearth the bleeding heifer is killed.
Let Roman wreaths be twined with Philetas' ivy.
From the spring of Callimachus let this urn be filled.
Give me sweet nard and offerings of incense;
three times around the hearth wind the fillet of wool;
sprinkle the water upon me; from the fresh altar
may the ancient music rise clear and beautiful.
Evil, be far off; find another homeland.
The laurel smooths the way that this priest must tread.
I shall tell of the temple of Palatine Apollo—
Calliope favors my theme with a nod of her head.
I sing my songs in honor of Caesar;[83] with Caesar
as subject, even Jove will hear what I say.
On the shores of Epirus, which is Apollo's country,
protected from wind and wave, is a little bay—
Actium, where Caesar's fleet was harbored
and storm-worn ship and sailor may find relief.
Here were the whole world's navies; they lay at anchor,
some of them fated for joy, some doomed to grief.
Egyptian and Roman: shameful that Roman weapons
should be hurled from those ships of Antony and the queen.
Caesar's are here, their sails filled with Jove's blessing,
as they fight for all that a fatherland can mean.
Now the sea god bends the line in a double crescent
and the water quivers under a shower of spears.
Apollo has left his island (it moves no more now,
though it used to float wherever the South Wind veers)
and has taken his place now over Caesar's flagship;
a triple flame of lightning shows where he stands.
This is not the god whose hair streams over his shoulders,

nor the god with a lyre of tortoise shell in his hands.
This is the face that looked on Agamemnon
and sent a plague to punish him for the rape
of Chryseis; this is the god the first of whose arrows
slew the Python, that hideous coiling shape.
"World-saver," he said, "descendant of Alba's founder,
greater than all your fathers who fled from Troy—
conquer the sea as the land. My bow fights for you;
for you is every arrow I employ.
Free your people from fear; they rely upon you;
the ships of your fleet are freighted with their prayer.
Defend our city, the city Romulus founded,
who watched while the birds of the Palatine took to the air.
The enemy's close—it is shameful that the Egyptian,
while you are prince, should sail so near these shores.
Do not fear. The sea will take none of those winged vessels,
though every one is rowed with a hundred oars,
though their prows are carved with figures like rock-hurling
    Centaurs—
they are painted terrors masking hollow planks.
If the cause is not just, men's hands will drop their weapons;
just cause can rally soldiers back to their ranks.
The time is now. Let your fleet be ready for launching—
I will guide your course with the laurel held in my hand."
He shot his arrows until the quiver was empty;
then came the shafts of the chief of Rome's command.
Apollo kept his promise; the queen, defeated,
watched the broken scepters float on the sea;
and the star-throned god, that earlier Caesar, marvelled,
"Who would doubt him blood of my blood, with this victory?"
Triton cheered, and the nymphs from the sea depths rising
clapped their hands for liberty's champion;

while the broken queen in her sloop fled back to Egypt
to choose the time for the setting of her sun.
It was heaven's plan; how would it have looked for a woman
to triumph through streets where Jugurtha himself was led?
And so we have given this temple to Apollo
who sank ten enemy ships with each arrow sped.
Enough of war. That Apollo whom we praise now
has put his armor aside for a peaceful dance.
Lay a rose wreath around my neck, and into the cool grove
let the banqueters in their snowy robes advance.
Brush the scent of saffron into my hair. Come,
press out the fresh sweet strong Falernian wine!
Bacchus, inspire Apollo as you love him;
Muses, send every poet his finest line—
tell how Augustus has conquered the Sycambi
and Africa, its sands by the hot winds blown;
how lately the Parthians, seeking truce, have yielded.
"They must give back Remus' standards or lose their own!
For whether Augustus seize it, or his grandsons
(should he leave such laurels to them), we shall win the East.
We shall reach your grave beyond the Euphrates, Crassus,
and your spirit, so long in exile, shall be released."

So this whole night of song and drinking is mine
till the sun's rays flash new brightness into the wine.

IV. vii

SUNT ALIQUID MANES; LETUM NON OMNIA FINIT . . .

There are ghosts after all, then; death is not the ending:
the soul, like smoke, escapes from the funeral flame.
Beside my bed I saw the wraith of Cynthia.
From that new grave by the noisy road she came
to me who, shaken, still, by the rites, lay restless
in the bed that was once our kingdom and was no more.
Her eyes, her hair, were the same as I had known them;
fire had charred one side of the robe she wore
and had eaten away the beryl ring on her finger;
her lips were withered from water drunk underground.
Her spirit, her voice, were living, but as she stood there
her brittle finger bones made a rattling sound.
"You forget so soon?" she said. "No woman ever
had a truer lover, yet sleep can erase the sight
of the little room we shared in the noisy Subura,
my window worn by ruses of the night,
the rope tossed over the sill where I'd hang for a moment
and hand over hand climb down into your embrace.
Under our cloaks the earth has been warmed by our bodies
as we lay by the crossroads in some shadowy place.
Our pledge was wordless, but our lies, our cheating,
the deaf southwestern wind has brushed away.
When I came to death, no man's voice called my name out,
though yours would have kept me alive another day;
for me no watchman troubled to sound his cleft reed;
a broken tile props up my fallen head.
Who has seen you stand by my grave grief-stricken?
who has seen your robe grow wet with the tears you shed?
If you could not bear to pass beyond my doorway,
could you not have begged them to carry me slowly here?

could you not have prayed for a wind to fan the flames high
or made them fragrant with nard? If you held me dear,
would a handful of hyacinths have been too costly
for my grave, or wine poured out of a broken urn?
It was Lygdamus the slave—I knew he was guilty
when I drank the wine. Let him feel the brand-iron burn!
As for Nomas, my woman, she may hide her poisons;
that burning jar will tell her crime to the town—
she, that cheap whore, that lowest of streetwalkers,
now trails in the dust the hem of her golden gown!
And if she hears that a slave has praised my beauty,
loads her shoulders with tasks she must faint beneath—
Petale's chained to a log, that poor old woman,
because she dared to bring to my grave a wreath;
Lalage's hung by her hair, whipped till she's bleeding,
for having asked Nomas a favor in my name.
And you—you let her melt down my golden image
to win her dowry from the fruit of that flame!
What reason I have to berate you!—yet I cannot;
in all your poems, it is my story you tell.
By the immutable chant of the Fates I swear it
(I tell the truth. Be silent, O dog of hell!):
I was faithful to you. If this is false, let adders
hiss on my tomb and coil through my bones, as well.
Beside the river of death there stand two mansions,
and to one or the other the dead must point the prow.
Adulterous Clytemnestra moves toward this one,
and Pasiphae in the wooden guise of the cow.
Toward the other in rose-decked boats go the blest, the godly,
where flowers are stirred by the softest airs of spring

and the air is full of the sound of harp and cymbal,
and turbaned dancers move to the plucked string.
Andromeda is there, and Hypermestre,
telling their stories of suffering and reward—
one as the scapegoat for her mother's boasting,
chained to the rock and rescued by Perseus' sword;
the other the single one of those fifty sisters
not guilty of murder on her wedding night.
Only death's tears can heal the wounds love dealt us;
I would hide your fickleness from all men's sight.
Listen—if your new mistress gives you leave to;
if you can hear my dead voice as I plead—
take care of my nurse Parthenie. You remember
she treated you well: see that she is not in need.
And that best of servants, Latris—do not expect her
to hold the mirror before your new love's face.
The poems you wrote to praise me—burn them, burn them.
Do not seek glory through my vanished grace.
But come to my tomb, and clear away the ivy
whose roots twist 'round my bones in a living mesh,
here where the Anio dawdles past the orchards
and ivory does not yellow, the air is so fresh.
Write a fitting phrase on some random pillar,
brief enough to catch the hurrying eye:
GOLDEN CYNTHIA LIES IN TIVOLI'S EARTH HERE:
NEW REASON TO HALLOW THIS LAND AND THE STREAM NEARBY.
You will have dreams, and you must learn to trust them;
through holy dreams the truth may be revealed.
At night we dead can wander—even Cerberus,
his chain cast off, will stray through forest and field,

until with dawn hell's law returns us to Lethe
where Charon the ferryman counts over his own.
Take your new love. I shall share you with no other
when you come to me here, and bone shall grind on bone."

And suddenly, her sad complaining ended,
she was gone, and I stood with my empty arms extended.

IV. viii

DISCE, QUID ESQUILIAS HAC NOCTE AQUOSAS . . .

You must hear of the panic last night in an Esquiline garden
that sent the neighbors fleeing in breakneck fear
when a noisy brawl broke out in one of the taverns
and blasted my name, though I swear I was nowhere near.
You know Lanuvium, that town to the southward
that a serpent guards; it's worth your while to inspect.
Food must be brought him through a darkening chasm
(on paths like that a girl must be circumspect)
as his yearly tribute, when he shows his hunger
by hisses that echo out of the earth's deep core.
Some girl must conquer her terror, stretch her hand forth
and put in those jaws the food he is waiting for.
From her tense fingers he snatches the offering; even
the baskets tremble on her trembling arm.
If she is a virgin, she comes home safe to her parents,
and the cry goes up, "Fine crops for every farm!"
Here Cynthia drove behind her close-clipped ponies,
for the rites of Juno, she said—of Venus, I'd guess.
The Appian Way could tell you of that journey
on whirling wheels—triumphant, regal, no less.
No eye could miss her, bending over the pole's end,
the horses never breaking their headlong stride.
(Who would note the silk-hung chariot of the pervert,
beardless and perfumed, with his dog at his side?—
proud now, but soon fit prey for a gladiator
to feed on, old and raddled and craving still . . .)
Why should I keep faith with the unfaithful?
she is away. I shall move my camp where I will.
There's Phyllis—she lives on the Aventine, near the temple;
sober, she's dreadful; liquor can lend her charms.
and Teia, in the Tarpeian groves; a beauty,

but one lover's not enough for her drunken arms.
So I called these two to come, lest I should be lonely—
it is always good to learn new ways to woo.
On a secret lawn we spread a couch for our pleasure:
a girl on each side, and I between the two.
Lygdamus served the wine in bowls of crystal—
summerware; there were tables and dice for bets.
An Egyptian piper played, and we all tossed roses
at pretty Phyllis, clacking the castanets;
Magnus the dwarf hopped to the flute music
on his shrunken stumps of legs like a clumsy ox—
when, from no lack of oil, the lamp flames flickered;
the table tottered and fell; when we shook the box
I kept drawing a six when an ace was what I needed;
the wine was suddenly sour in my mouth;
I looked unmoved at their breasts, was deaf to their singing—
I stood at Lanuvium's gate, alone, far south.
And then without warning the outer door's hinges were creaking
and I heard light feet come running across the court.
She flung herself on us like some raging fury,
a beauty now of a new and different sort.
I dropped my cup; my wine-flushed face grew pallid;
her eyes could have been great Jupiter's thunderbolts
and we a city sacked. She scratched at Phyllis
till the two girls ran from the place like frightened colts—
calling the neighbors, screeching, waving lanterns,
all dishevelled, they fled to a tavern nearby.
Exultant, Cynthia chased them, and then, returning,
slapped my face (you can see where the red welts rise),
bit my neck till it bore her bloody toothmarks,
and made a fist and blacked my guilty eyes.

Then, weary with beating me, she routed Lygdamus
who had hidden there to our left far under the bed.
She dragged him upright, yelping with apprehension—
though he shouted for help, I was shielding my own head.
Finally I gave in and knelt like a captive,
but she would not let me so much as touch her feet,
saying, "If you expect me to forgive you,
these are the terms that I expect you to meet:
No more parading the streets to be admired;
no displaying your wealth at gladiatorial shows;
no craning your neck toward the gallery at the theater;
no peering in litters whenever a curtain blows.
Last and most important, sell Lygdamus.
I hate him. Shackle his feet; put him up for sale."
I said, "I accept the terms," and she laughed in my face then,
knowing her power over me could not fail.
With fire she purified what the girls had handled,
washed the place free from any sign of their crimes,
ordered me to change every stitch of my clothing,
with burning sulphur touched my head three times,
and at last, imperious, let herself be taken
on that fresh-made bed she never should have forsaken.

IV. ix

AMPHITRYONIADES QUA TEMPESTATE IUVENCOS . . .

When Hercules had driven Geryon's cattle
eastward from Erythia, he made his way
to a hill unheld by men, where sheep were grazing—
the Palatine—and where the marshes lay
at its foot, with the winding river lost in the marshes,
he halted to rest near a cave and a little grove.
But Cacus, his host, betrayed the faith put in him—
Cacus the thief whose theft would outrage Jove.
He was a robber who made his cave an ambush;
three-headed, he had three voices to make men quail;
and cunningly, lest there be a track to follow,
he dragged the oxen backward by the tail.
But Jove had seen, and, led by the sound of the lowing,
Hercules broke through the door with its trophies of bone,
lifted up his Arcadian club and swung it
three times round to leave the robber prone.
Then he spoke to the oxen: "Go, last of my labors;
twice I searched for you, twice you were my prey.
Where you stand and bellow shall be the Place of Oxen—
shall be the Roman Forum, some distant day."
When he finished, his tongue was parched and his lips burning,
but the marsh was muddy water; he saw no spring—
and then he heard the laughter of women, sheltered
in a dark and holy grove, and murmuring
in that secret place, the shrine of the Good Goddess,[84]
with its sacred fountains and rites no man has seen.
Across the secluded gates were veils of purple;
incense made the small hut seem less mean.
Over the shrine the leaves of a poplar quivered,
and out of them came the song of a thousand birds.
Here he rushed, his beard all matted and dusty,

breaking in with hoarse and unfitting words:
"In this consecrated grove where you praise your goddess,
I pray you, open the fane. I am not a spy,
but parched with thirst in a country noisy with waters—
cup some fresh in your hands, let me drink, or I die.
You know of the man who balanced the world on his shoulders?
I am Hercules to that world I once held high.
All ears have heard the stories of my cudgel
and the tales of my arrows that never miss their mark.
Receive me here. This land does not pity the weary,
even one for whom hell's pathways were not dark.
You are sacrificing to Juno? My stepmother—
but she would not close the waters to anyone.
Are you frightened by my cloak with its head of a lion,
or my face and my hair burned black by the African sun?
Do not fear. I have been a slave in eastern countries
and worked the wool like a girl at the spinning wheel.
Though my chest is hairy, I covered it like a maiden,
and my hands were nimble, however rough to feel."
He ended his plea, and the kindly priestess answered,
her white hair bound around with a purple band:
"Stranger, you must not stay; this place is hallowed.
Do not profane it. Escape to another land.
The shrine in this hidden hut where we serve the goddess
is forbidden to men; at their peril they have spied.
Tiresias paid the price for watching Minerva
bathing, her Gorgon breastplate laid aside.
Let the gods find you other fountains. In its channel
this virginal stream flows far from the paths of man."
But as she spoke, his fist struck out at the shut door;
driven by thirst, straight into the shrine he ran,

and when he had drunk the water down to the stream bed,
he made his decree from lips that were not yet dry:
"This land does not pity the weary; yet this corner
of the world receives me; here I wait to die.
May that other altar at the Place of Oxen[85]
which my hands have built to be the greatest, the first—
may that be closed forever to any woman
so that she will remember how I have avenged my thirst."

Hail, Hercules—a god, and in Juno's graces!
bless this your story, and see that it endures.
Because you cleansed the world and made it holy,
the Sabines built this temple and called it yours.

IV. x

NUNC IOVIS INCIPIAM CAUSAS APERIRE FERETRI . . .

Shall I tell you why we surname Jove Feretrius?
because on him the spoils of war are conferred—
the plunder taken by Romulus from Latium
first, and the loot of a second chief, and a third.
A difficult theme: grant me power to try it.
                                    The founder
of Rome was the first who brought war's booty home
when his spear sent Acron, the Sabines' ally, reeling
from his horse as he galloped toward the gates of Rome—
Acron, descendant of Hercules, king of Caenina,
whose name all Romans once had reason to dread.
He dreamed of killing Romulus with one swordthrust,
but his own life blood it was that ran, instead.
Romulus saw the javelin poised for hurling,
saw it, and won Jove's blessing with a vow:
"Lord of Olympus, let Acron fall in your honor!"
You can see those trophies here in this temple now.
He was in the habit of winning, our founder and teacher;
trained to hardihood through a rigorous youth,
he could guide a plow as readily as a war horse;
though his helmet was plumed, it was only wolfskin, in truth;
his solid shield could not boast any bronze inlay;
the belt at his side was cut from a cow's tough hide.
We warred on a small scale, then—Nomentum and Cora;
we had not yet fought on the Tiber's further side.

The second hero is Cossus, who killed Tolumnius
when the conquest of Veii seemed a fantastic dream—
ancient Veii, vanished now as a kingdom,
in whose market place a gold throne used to gleam,
from your broken walls the shepherd's shrill horn echoes;
cornfields grow where the bones of your people are laid.

Tolumnius stood on the portal tower of Veii,
carrying on the parley, unafraid.
While the ram's horn shook the walls with its brassy blaring
and the breastworks of the besiegers covered their line,
Cossus cried out, "Brave men fight in the open!"
and the two marched forth as though by the gods' design—
but the gods had chosen Cossus; the head of his rival,
struck off, has spattered the Roman horses with blood.

And Claudius third, with the shield of the barbarian,
when the Belgians crossed where the Rhone's wild waters flood—
that shield of Virdomarus, the Rhine's own offspring
whose chariot never swerved as he flung his spear.
In trousers woven with stripes he faced the Romans;
from his severed head was taken this helmet here.

In Jupiter's temple is all the loot of these leaders—
Jove the Conferrer of Help when his aid was sought;
Jove, to whom were offered the spoils and the trophies
that the victor, his shoulders bent by the burden, brought.

IV. xi

DESINE, PAULLE, MEUM LACRIMIS URGERE SEPULCRUM . . .

Paullus, your grief weighs down the earth above me.[87]
It is useless, love; no prayer moves these black gates.
Once we come to this kingdom, we are captives—
the walls of hell are adamant as the Fates.
Though Pluto may hear your pleading here in the darkness,
the Styx will drink your tears and show no sign.
Prayers move the gods; these doors clang shut on shadows
when Charon has taken the toll, as he took mine.
This is the meaning of those wailing trumpets
when fire consumed the couch where my body lay.
Nothing could save me—not our love, our marriage,
ancestral glory, our children who mourn today:
they could not keep Cornelia from her dying.
What am I now but dust that a hand could hold?
Black doom and shallow pools of stagnant water
and the streams I walk through, silent and icy-cold,
you know I come here innocent and unready.
God of the darkness,[88] grant me your dark grace!
Or, if Aeacus sit with his urn beside him,
let him find by lot what punishment I must face.
Let Minos and Rhadamanthus and the Furies
join him as judges. Tell the court, "Be still."
Let the stone roll back, and the wheel stop for an hour,
and the dusty lips of Tantalus drink their fill.
For one day, Cerberus, do not attack your victims,
while the chain hangs slack and quiet from the bar.
If I speak falsehood, send me to join the Danaids
and carry water, like them, in a leaking jar.
Does ancient lineage gain its recognition?
Africa's conquest was my father's boast;
my mother's family was no less distinguished—

each name upholds our house like a solid post.
I was born to this, and when the wreath of marriage
caught up my hair, and I was a woman grown,
it was your bed, my Paullus, that I came to
and now have left. The carving on the stone
says, SHE WED BUT ONCE. O fathers long respected,
victors in Africa, be my defense . . .
and Perseus, proud of great Achilles' kinship
and his who broke through hell's bleak battlements:
I asked no favors when Paullus was made censor;
no evil found its way within our walls.
I do not think I have disgraced my fathers;
I set a decent pattern in these halls.
Days had a quiet rhythm; no scandal touched us
from the wedding torch to the torch beside my bier.
A certain integrity is proof of breeding:
the love of virtue should not be born of fear.
Whoever the judge, whatever the lot fate gives me,
no woman needs to blush who sits at my side—
not Cybele's priestess, Claudia, pulling to safety
the boat with the holy image, caught in the tide;
not the Vestal who swore by her robe she would rekindle
the fire they said she had left, and the ash blazed flame;
and most of all not you, my mother, Scribonia—
all but the way of my death you would have the same.
Your grief and the grief of Rome ennoble my spirit;
the tears of Caesar protect my soul in hell.
He mourns for me, half-sister to his daughter—
among men's tears, a god may weep as well.
For my children I wore the mother's robe of honor;

it was no empty house I left behind.
Lepidus, Paullus, still you bring me comfort:
you closed my eyes when death had made them blind.
Twice in the curule chair[89] I have seen my brother;
they cheered him as consul the day before I died.
And you, my daughter, ideal of your censor-father,
choose one husband and live content at his side:
our clan will rest on the children that you give it.
Secure in their promise, I board the boat and rejoice.
Mine is the final triumph of any woman,
that her spirit earn the praise of a living voice.
Paullus, I leave you as pledge of my love our children:
guard them; this care still burns in my dead heart.
Their hands seek yours; their arms lie round your shoulders.
You must take a father's and now a mother's part.
When you kiss their tear-streaked faces, add my kisses.
The house, the whole house, darling, needs your care.
Weep for me—but I beg, let no one see you,
the children least of all guess your despair.
Long haunted nights—how many of them wait you,
with dreams to break the heart and trick the eye.
O when you speak in secret to my phantom,
say every word as though I would reply.
And if our bed in the atrium grows too lonely,
so that a new wife comes to take my place—
dear sons, make her feel welcome; praise her virtues,
proving your own, and do it with good grace.
Mention me rarely. It may rouse her anger
if she and I are constantly compared,
and to her detriment. If he seeks no solace
save days remembered from the life we shared—

as he grows older, let him not be lonely;
sorrows lie heavy enough upon him now.
I would add to yours the years that fate took from me:
love him I love, whose body age will bow.
It is well with me: I wore no robes of mourning;
you come to my tomb, my dear ones, all of you.
I plead no more. Witnesses, rise from sorrow;
a welcoming earth will grant my life its due.

My fathers live in light; the gods reward them.
If I deserve such grace, then bear me toward them.

STUDIES OF PROPERTIUS

Recommended for Further Reading

BUTLER, H. E. and BARBER, E. A. *The Elegies of Propertius*. Oxford: Clarendon Press, 1933.

CAMPS, W. A. *Propertius, Elegies, Book I*. Cambridge, England: University Press, 1961.

DAMON, P. W. and HELMBOLD, W. C. *The Structure of Propertius, Book 2*. University of California Publications in Classical Philology. Berkeley, California: 1952. Volume 14, No. 6, pp. 215-254.

FONTENROSE, JOSEPH. *Propertius and the Roman Career*. University of California Publications in Classical Philology. Berkeley, California: 1949. Volume 13, No. 11, pp. 371-388.

HIGHET, GILBERT. "Life Behind the Ivy," *Horizon*, III (January, 1961), pp. 117-119.

————. *Poets in a Landscape*. New York: Knopf, 1957.

LUCK, GEORG. *The Latin Love-Elegy*. New York: Barnes and Noble, 1960.

POSTGATE, J. P. *Select Elegies of Propertius*. London: Macmillan, 1950.

SELLAR, W. Y. *The Roman Poets of the Augustan Age*. Oxford: Clarendon Press, 1891. Volume I: "Horace and the Elegiac Poets."

SULLIVAN, J. P. "Cynthia Prima Fuit: A Causerie," *Arion*, I (Autumn, 1962), pp. 34-44.

NOTES

1. *No trickery won for Leucippus' daughters the heart of Pollux, or his brother's heart.* See LEUCIPPUS in glossary.

2. *Jason's bride.* Medea. See glossary.

3. *He who died first at Troy.* Protesilaus, a Greek commander. His wife so mourned for him that the gods let her see him for three hours.

4. *Theiodamus' son.* See THEIODAMUS in glossary.

5. *Giant's strand.* The Phlegrean Plains. See glossary.

6. *Wars of Jove and Giant.* See GIANTS in glossary.

7. *the breastplate that had made men stone.* The breastplate of Minerva showed the head of Medusa with snaky locks; upon seeing it, men were turned to stone. See GORGONS in glossary.

8. *Pirithous' bride.* See PIRITHOUS in glossary.

9. *You maids who build to Chastity her temples.* No special reference. It just means, "Once you are married, oh maidens, you abandon chastity as an ideal."

10. *The law's repealed at last.* The law that would have forced Propertius to marry within his station and abandon Cynthia. After Cynthia's death, Propertius probably did marry. Pliny refers to a person from Assisi who claimed Propertius as a direct ancestor.

11. *Theban chieftains fought.* Polynices and Eteocles, sons of Oedipus, contested for the rule of Thebes. See THEBAN SEVEN in glossary.

12. *Parthia's role in it.* See note 35.

13. *her who once betrayed him.* Apparently a reference to Semele. See glossary.

14. *Phrygian mountain.* Mount Sipylus in Phrygia, where Niobe sat weeping when she was turned into stone. See NIOBE in glossary.

15. *another king*. Creon, king of Corinth, whose daughter Creusa became the bride of Jason. See CREUSA in glossary.

16. *goddess once a heifer*. Io. See glossary.

17. *virgin goddess*. Vesta. See glossary.

18. *Sisters*. The Sirens. See glossary.

19. *how to Troy's towers he flew once, as a bird*. A reference to Jupiter carrying off Ganymede, Jupiter being represented here as the actual eagle that swooped down and carried the handsome Ganymede to heaven.

20. *sacred ivy wreath*. The wreath worn in Bacchic revels.

21. *Apollo's golden colonnade*. Propertius refers to the porticoes of the new temple of Apollo on the Palatine, vowed in 36 B.C. and dedicated October 9, 28 B.C. by Augustus. It symbolized Augustus' victory over Pompey in 36 B.C. and later his victory over Antony and Cleopatra in 31 B.C. With Apollo as its figurehead, the temple also symbolized the new cultural tastes and ambitions of Augustan art by including a library, connected to the adjoining porticoes that Propertius describes here. In the *Epistle to Florus*, Horace pictures himself and an elegiac poet (presumably Propertius), standing in front of the new library complimenting each other on their poetic talents.

22. *how the Gauls were hurled from Delphi*. A reference to the attack on Delphi by the Gauls under Brennus in 278 B.C. They were driven off by storm and earthquake.

23. *how Tantalus' daughter came to die*. A reference to Niobe. See glossary.

24. *Tyndareus' daughter ran off with a stranger*. A reference to Helen of Troy. See glossary.

25. *how Mars was lusted for by Venus*. The seduction is described by Homer in *Odyssey* XV.

26. *Minos' queen*. Pasiphae. See glossary.

27. *this ceremony*. The rites of Isis. See glossary.

28. *stranger's wife*. That is, as the bride of Jason, who took her back to Greece from Colchis. See MEDEA in glossary.

29. *Vergil*. Propertius expresses his admiration for Vergil's work-in-progress, the *Aeneid*, hailing it as greater than the *Iliad*:

cedite Romani scriptores, cedite Grai!

nescio quid maius nascitur Iliade.

30. *Muses' mountain.* Mount Helicon. See glossary.

31. *O Nine.* The Muses. See glossary.

32. *river god.* Achelous. See glossary.

33. *Marcian stream.* The Aqua Marcia. See note 69; also MARCIA in glossary.

34. *Jove saved by the cackling of a goose.* A reference to the attack on the Capitoline by the Gauls in 367 B.C. The Romans were alerted by the cackling of the sacred geese in the precincts of the temple of Jupiter Optimus Maximus.

35. *German horde.* A reference to the Teutons, who were defeated by Marius in 102 B.C.

36. *the spring wherein Philetas found delight.* The Castalian spring, a source of poetic inspiration. See PHILETAS in glossary.

37. *On Parthia now Caesar our god plans warfare.* See PARTHIA in glossary.

38. *the pearl-bearing sea.* The Indian Ocean.

39. *gods of Parthia's world.* A reference to emblems from Parthia, signifying Rome's eventual victory over her. See PARTHIA in glossary.

40. *Corinth's burning.* An allusion to Corinthian bronze, said to have been formed by the accidental fusing of gold, silver, and bronze at the burning of Corinth by Mummius in 146 B.C.

41. *Ulysses' beggar.* Irus, the beggar with whom Ulysses fought when he returned home.

42. *why the sun's horses went in dark-robed mourning.* A general reference (purely literary) to earthquakes in mountainous districts.

43. *lake-bound thirsting.* A reference to the punishment of Tantalus. See glossary.

44. *seven fights.* See THEBAN SEVEN in glossary.

45. *Jove-burned citadel.* Jupiter came to Semele in the guise of a thunderbolt, and she was, of course, killed. See SEMELE in glossary.

46. *returning of the Greek ships that tenth year.* The Greeks pretended to sail away from Troy, leaving the wooden horse behind them; then they returned secretly.

47. *twins wolf-nurtured.* The reference is to Romulus and Remus.

48. *false Parthians who fled.* The Parthians were well known for

their ability to shoot arrows back over their shoulders when they were apparently escaping in full flight.

49. *Pelusium's camp conquered by Roman power.* See PELUSIUM in glossary.

50. *Persia's city.* Babylon. See glossary.

51. *her who mocked our armies.* Cleopatra. See glossary.

52. *his three triumphs.* A reference to the military successes of Pompey. See glossary.

53. *Ptolemy's queen.* Cleopatra, who was the wife of her brother Ptolemy before Julius Caesar aided her to win the supreme power in Egypt. See CLEOPATRA in glossary.

54. *sacred asps.* A reference to the asps which Cleopatra allowed to bite her when she wished to commit suicide. See CLEOPATRA in glossary.

55. *blind giant.* Polyphemus the Cyclops, who was blinded by Ulysses on his return voyage from the Trojan War (in the *Odyssey*).

56. *The ant brings gold dust and the Indian steals it.* Both Pliny and Herodotus assert that somewhere in India gold dust was brought from underground by ants in wintertime, and in the summer stolen by the Indians, after the ants had retired to their nests because of the heat.

57. *Tyrian purple.* Phoenician purple dye was most famous. Tyre was a Phoenician city.

58. *a war he knew could not be won.* A reference to Amphiarus, who foresaw his own doom; he was one of the Seven against Thebes. See AMPHIARUS in glossary; also THEBAN SEVEN.

59. *Amazonian warriors bathing.* The Amazons were women warriors, who bathed in the Thermodon, a river in Cappadocia.

60. *you have your love.* A reference to Ariadne. See glossary.

61. *horned god.* Bacchus pictured as a Satyr. See BACCHUS in glossary.

62. *one Jove blasted.* A reference to Semele. See glossary.

63. *how Indian warriors fled from Nysa's bands.* The worship of Bacchus which originated in the Middle East and overcame its antagonists as it moved westward to invade Greece. See NYSA in glossary.

64. *Tuscan sailors, turned dolphins.* Some sailors who were escorting Bacchus tried to kidnap him, so he turned them into dolphins.

65. *Hercules' road.* The strip of land sheltering the Lucrine lake from the sea. It was said to have been built by Hercules when he returned with the cattle of Geryon. See GERYON in glossary.

66. *Trumpeter of Troy.* Misenus, Aeneas' trumpeter, buried on Cape Misenus near Cumae.

67. *Isthmus.* The land connecting northern and southern Greece.

68. *Thesean road.* The approach to Athens. Theseus, the first historical king of Athens, took this route on his return from Crete.

69. *rocks' cruel test.* A reference to the voyage of the Argo through the Clashing Rocks (Symplegades). See ARGO in glossary.

70. *seven-channelled river.* The Nile river in Egypt.

71. *Marcian conduit.* The famous aqueduct celebrated for the excellence of its water, The Aqua Marcia, built by Q. Marcius Rex in 144 B.C.

72. *Alba's lake, and . . . Nemi.* Two volcanic lakes.

73. *sun god shocked by Atreus' banqueting.* The reference is to the meal prepared for Thyestes by Atreus. The sun turned back his chariot in horror at the deed. See ATREUS in glossary.

74. *No girl need die so that a fleet may sail.* A reference to the sacrifice of Iphigenia by her father, Agamemnon. See IPHIGENIA in glossary.

75. *Juno would change no maiden to a heifer. . . .* A reference to Io. See glossary.

76. *ships, lured by false beacons.* A reference to the destruction wrought by Nauplius. See NAUPLIUS in glossary.

77. *Ascanius' Alba. . . .* Here and in the following lines Propertius refers to the legend of Rome's foundation in Vergil's *Aeneid*.

78. *holy hill.* The Aventine hill in Rome, a place of shrines and sanctuaries.

79. *Drunken Ajax rapes the holy priestess.* Ajax raped Cassanda. See AJAX in glossary.

80. *child of the Crab.* The allusion is to Cynthia's avarice. Those born under the sign of the Crab were supposed to be avaricious.

81. *Terra Tuum Spinis Obducat, Lena, Sepulchrum*. An invective poem against the procuress (*lena*) Acanthis, now dead, who corrupted the mind of Propertius' unnamed mistress.

82. *Dear love, dear life*. Propertius cites the first two lines of the second elegy of Book I. These lines may have been inserted later, long after Propertius' death.

83. *in honor of Caesar*. Propertius' "Actium Ode" probably was written for the annual festival celebrating Augustus' triumph over Antony and Cleopatra.

84. *Good Goddess*. The Bona Dea, goddess of women.

85. *Place of Oxen*. The Forum Boarium, where the Ara Maxima of Hercules were. Hercules took the cattle of Geryon and drove them to Greece. See HERCULES and GERYON in glossary.

86. *Jove Feretrius*. See JUPITER FERETRIUS in glossary.

87. *your grief*. This is a reference to the grief of L. Aemilius Paullus Lepidus for his dead wife Cornelia. This "funeral oration" is spoken by Cornelia herself.

88. *God of darkness*. See PLUTO in glossary.

89. *curule chair*. Official chair of consuls, praetors, and curule aediles.

NAME-PLACE GLOSSARY

ACADEMIA. The school of philosophy in Athens founded by Plato.

ACANTHIS. The bawd (*lena*) whose cunning instruction of Cynthia in the "art of love" enrages Propertius.

ACHELOUS. A river in Greece. As a personified deity, Achelous wrestled with Hercules for Deianira.

ACHILLES. The greatest Greek warrior in the Trojan war; slayer of Hector. Achilles' mother, Thetis, dipped him in the river Styx and so made him invulnerable except for one place on his heel.

ACRON. King of Caenina killed in combat by Romulus, who bore off the "richest spoils" in combat (*spolia opima*) and dedicated them to Jupiter "the Bearer" (*Feretrius*). (See JUPITER FERETRIUS.)

ACTIUM. A promontory on the coast of Epirus where Augustus defeated Antony and Cleopatra in a sea battle in 31 B.C.

ADONIS. Greek youth loved by Venus and mourned for at his untimely death.

ADRASTUS. Leader of the Seven Against Thebes. (See THEBAN SEVEN.)

AEACUS. A judge of the dead.

AEMILIUS. Aemilius Paulus, who defeated Demetrius of Pherae in 219 B.C.

AENEAS. Trojan hero of Vergil's *Aeneid*. He voyaged to Italy and laid the foundations of the Roman empire.

AESCHYLUS. The great Greek tragedian (525-546 B.C.).

AETNA. Volcanic mountain in Sicily.

AGAMEMNON. Commander of the Greek forces in the Trojan War.

AJAX. One of the Greek heroes who participated in the Trojan War, second only to Achilles in might. He raped Cassandra and was punished by the gods.

ALBA. A colony founded by the descendants of Aeneas before the foundation of Rome, in the hilly range (hence Alba Longa) twenty miles southeast of Rome.

ALCINOUS. King of luxurious Phaeacia, who gave Ulysses rich gifts.

ALCMAEON. (1) He killed his mother and was pursued by the Furies. (2) The husband of Alphesiboea. (See ALPHESIBOEA.)

ALCMENA. The wife of Amphitryon and mother of Hercules, Jupiter being the father.

ALEXANDRIA. Cultural and commercial capital of the Greek world from the third century B.C. on. The Roman general Pompey was traitorously murdered here near the end of the Civil War, in 48 B.C.

ALEXIS. A shepherd mentioned in Vergil's *Eclogues*.

ALPHESIBOEA. The wife of Alcmaeon, who left her for Callirhoe. Alphesiboea's brothers killed Alcmaeon for this unfaithfulness, but Alphesiboea avenged her husband by killing her brothers.

AMPHIARAUS. A seer, one of the Seven against Thebes, who knowingly went to his doom when his chariot was swallowed up in a chasm. (See THEBAN SEVEN.)

AMPHION. Twin brother of Zethus. (See ANTIOPE.)

AMYMONE. A daughter of Danaus, who yielded to Neptune, on condition that he make a spring rise up in time of drought.

ANCHISES. The father of Aeneas; Venus was Aeneas' mother.

ANDROGEON. Son of Minos, slain in Attica; but, according to Propertius, he was restored to life by Asclepius (in Homer, a physician; later the Greek god of healing).

ANDROMEDA. A mythological princess of Ethiopia, chained to a rock by the sea shore to appease a sea monster, but rescued by Perseus.

ANIO. A river rising in the Sabine hills and flowing seventy-five miles west-southwest, past Tivoli, to join the Tiber at Antemnae just north of Rome.

ANTAEUS. The Libyan giant who could not be overthrown so long as he kept contact with the earth. Hercules lifted him into the air until the giant's strength failed.

ANTIGONE. The daughter of Oedipus, condemned to death by Creon. Haemon, Creon's son, committed suicide when he discovered that Antigone had killed herself in the cave where she was confined.

ANTIMACHUS. A Greek poet of Colophon (ca. 444 B.C.) who wrote an epic on the Seven against Thebes (see THEBAN SEVEN). He also wrote love elegies in memory of his mistress Lyde.

ANTINOUS. The chief suitor of Penelope in the *Odyssey*.

ANTIOPE. Replaced by Dirce in the affections of her husband Lycus, and ultimately protected by her sons Amphion and Zethus, who killed Dirce by tying her to the horns of a bull. In III.xv Propertius examines the motive for Dirce's jealousy and Antiope's revenge.

ANTONY. Marcus Antonius, Roman general, first the ally of Augustus, then his rival for the supreme power. He had many military successes—Mo-

dena, Philippi, Pharsala, Parthia—before he met Cleopatra. (See CLEO-
PATRA.)

APOLLO. Greek god, patron of arts; born on island of Delos; guardian
deity of the battle of Actium, where the hill became sacred to him
(IV. 1).

APELLES. Greek painter, from the island of Cos (fourth century B.C.).

APPIAN WAY. A famous Roman road (*regina viarum*), from Rome to Naples, main route to southern Italy, begun by Appius Claudius in 312 B.C.

ARABY. The whole region of Arabia and Persia.

ARCADIA. A mountainous region in southern Greece; later associated with
pastoral poetry as its land of bliss.

ARCHEMORUS. Infant son of Eurydice and Lycurgus, king of Nemea. He
was killed by a serpent and the funeral games in his honor gave rise to
the Nemean Games.

ARCTURUS. The brightest star in Bootes; or, the whole constellation. (See
ICARUS.)

ARETHUSA. Perhaps pseudonym for Aelia Galla (III.xii). This imaginary
letter from a Roman lady to her husband (Lycotas, perhaps a pseudonym for Postumus) absent on military service may have influenced
Ovid in the composition of his *Heroides* (written between 19 and 2
B.C.).

ARGO. The ship built by the Greek heroes to carry them on the quest for
the Golden Fleece. (See GOLDEN FLEECE.)

ARGUS. The thousand-eyed creature ordered by Juno to guard Io. (See IO.)

ARGYNNUS. A beautiful Boeotian boy beloved of Agamemnon; drowned
in the Cephisus river in Boeotia, and given burial by Agememnon.

ARIADNE. Cretan princess taken from Crete by Theseus but abandoned by
him on the island of Naxos and subsequently taken to heaven by Bacchus to be his bride. Ariadne made it possible for Theseus to penetrate
the Labyrinth, slay the Minotaur, and escape.

ARION. (1) The horse of Adrastus, gifted with human speech. (2) A famous Greek poet (ca. 625 B.C.); returning to Corinth from Sicily, he
was thrown overboard by the sailors but rescued by a dolphin.

ARRIA. A friend or kinswoman of Propertius.

ARTEMIS. Identical with Diana. (See DIANA.)

ASCANIUS. (1) The son of Aeneas. (2) A river in Asia Minor.

ASCRA. The birthplace of the poet Hesiod in Boeotia.

ASCRAEUS. The Roman poets frequently used the adjective "Ascraeus" in
the sense of Hesiodic, i.e., a reference to the poet Hesiod. Vergil did this
in *Georgics* II. 176. (See ASCRA).

ASSISI. Hill town in Umbria, probably the ancient Asis which Propertius mentions as his native town.

ATALANTA. Mythological Arcadian princess, fast enough in running to outdistance suitors who competed for her hand. Milanion, or Hippomenes, threw in her path the three golden apples he had received from Venus, and thus he overtook Atalanta.

ATHENS. The capital city of Attica, in Greece.

ATLAS. The Titan who held up the heavens. (See TITANS.)

ATREUS. The father of Agamemnon. He served Thyestes a banquet of the limbs of his sons, after Thyestes had made Atreus, unknowingly, slay his own son, Pleisthenes.

ATTIC. Pertaining to Attica, in Greece.

AUGUSTUS. This title was conferred on the Roman chief of state (*princeps*) by decree of the Senate on January 16, 27 B.C. Augustus was originally named Gaius Octavius; in the will left by Julius Caesar he was nominated as Caesar's chief heir, and in 43 B.C. he was recognized as Caesar's adopted son under the name of Gaius Julius Caesar Octavianus. The title "Augustus" was held by all subsequent Roman emperors except Vitellius, and never by any other member of the imperial family.

AULIS. A seaport in Greece where the Greek fleet gathered before sailing for Troy. Agamemnon sacrificed his daughter Iphigenia at Aulis.

AURORA. The goddess of the dawn.

BABYLON. Ancient capital of the south Semitic kingdom of Mesopotamia on the Euphrates river.

BACCHANTES. Ecstatic female worshippers of Bacchus.

BACCHUS. The god of wine.

BACTRIA. The general region of the Middle Oxus, a fertile irrigated land.

BAIA. A seaside resort near Naples. Legend attributes the causeway to Hercules.

BASSUS. A friend of Propertius and writer of iambic poetry.

BOREAS. The North Wind, personified as a winged deity.

BOSPORUS. "Ox-ford," the place where Io is alleged to have crossed the water at a narrow strait joining the Black Sea to the Mediterranean and dividing Asia and Europe. (See IO.)

BOVILLAE. A small town just outside Rome.

BRENNUS. The Gallic chieftain who attacked Delphi in 278 B.C.

BRIMO. Hecate in her nymph aspect, equivalent to Persephone. (See PERSEPHONE.)

BRISEIS. The mistress of Achilles in the *Iliad*.

BRUTUS. Lucius Junius Brutus, whose consulship in 509 B.C. signifies the end of the rule of the kings.

CACUS. A gigantic robber slain by Hercules for stealing his cattle near the Palatine hill in Rome and hiding them in a cave on the Aventine hill.

CAENINA. Small town in Latium; its king, Acron, was killed by Romulus in an engagement stemming from the rape of the Sabine women. (See SABINE RAPE.)

CAESAR. Julius Caesar in III.xviii and IV.vi; elsewhere in Propertius, Gaius Julius Caesar Octavianus Augustus. (See AUGUSTUS.)

CALAIS. Winged son of the North Wind (Boreas).

CALAMIS. Fifth-century Greek sculptor who specialized in horses.

CALCHAS. The Greek soothsayer who advised Agamemnon to sacrifice his daughter Iphigenia at Aulis.

CALLIMACHUS. The famous Alexandrian scholar-poet (ca. 250 B.C.) whose work influenced Catullus and Propertius.

CALLIOPE. The muse of epic poetry.

CALLISTO. A nymph of Arcadia transformed into the constellation of the Little Bear.

CALVUS. G. Licinius Calvus, friend of Catullus and fellow poet of the Alexandrian school.

CALYPSO. A nymph who loved Ulysses and detained him on her island of Ogygia.

CAMILLUS. Marcus Furius Camillus, a famous early Roman leader and second founder of Rome after the Gallic invasion in 387 B.C.

CAMPANIA. The region of Italy surrounding Naples, bounded on the north by Capua and on the south by Sorrento.

CANNAE. The scene of a battle in which Hannibal the Carthaginian defeated the Romans in southern Italy in 216 B.C.

CAPANEUS. One of the Seven against Thebes (see THEBAN SEVEN). He defied Jove and was killed by a thunderbolt.

CAPITOLINE. The hill in Rome on which stood the largest temple of Jupiter.

CAPRICORN. The tenth sign of the zodiac, represented by a goat, or a figure with its fore part like a goat and its hind part like a fish. The sun enters Capricorn at the winter solstice.

CARTHAGE. Rome's chief early rival for power in the Mediterranean, a city on the coast of North Africa near modern Tunis, finally destroyed by the Romans in 146 B.C.

CASSANDRA. Victimized priestess of Apollo in the Trojan War; her true prophecies were not believed. Agamemnon took her back to Greece as his concubine, and there she was killed by Clytemnestra.

CASTOR. The equestrian athlete, brother of Helen of Troy; deified with his twin brother Pollux, the boxing athlete.

CATHAY. The general region of China and the Far East.

CATULLUS. The famous Roman lyric poet, Gaius Valerius Catullus (ca. 84-54 B.C.).

CENTAUR. A tribe of mythological creatures with the upper part of a human being and the lower part of a horse.

CERBERUS. The three-headed watchdog of Hades.

CHARON. The boatman who carries the dead across the river Styx to Hades.

CHARYBDIS. A dangerous maelstrom in a narrow channel of water, usually thought of as opposite Scylla. (See SCYLLA.)

CHIOS. A Greek island in the Aegean, famous for its wine and figs.

CHRYSEIS. The daughter of the priest Chryses in the *Iliad*. Agamemnon was compelled to return her to her father and thereupon took the girl Briseis from Achilles.

CIMBRIA. A region in Germany.

CIRCE. A goddess who had the magical power to turn men into beasts (in the *Odyssey*.)

CITHAERON. A mountain between Attica and Boeotia.

CLAUDIUS. Marcus Marcellus Claudius, the conqueror of Syracuse in 211 B.C. Earlier, at Clastidium in 222 B.C., he killed the Gallic chieftain Virdomarus in single combat and thereby won the *spolia opima*.

CLEOPATRA. Queen of Egypt (69-30 B.C.). With the aid of Julius Caesar, she won power in Egypt, then becoming Caesar's mistress and the mother of his son Caesarion. Later Marc Antony became her lover. In the battle of Actium (31 B.C.) Octavian defeated Cleopatra and Antony, who both committed suicide.

CLITUMNUS. A small river in Umbria, springing from a rock in a grove of cypress trees.

CLYTEMNESTRA. The wife of Agamemnon; she killed him upon his returning home from the Trojan War.

CONON. A Greek astronomer (ca. 259 B.C.).

CORA. A hill town of the Volscians, an ancient Italian tribe eventually conquered by the Romans under Gnaeus Marcius "Coriolanus."

CORINNA. Boeotian poetess, contemporary with Pindar (early sixth century B.C.).

CORINTH. The isthmus city between northern Greece and the Peloponnesus.

CORNELIA. The daughter of Cornelius Scipio and Scribonia, and the wife of L. Aemilius Paullus.

CORYDON. A shepherd mentioned in Vergil's *Eclogues*.

COSSUS. Aulus Cornelius Cossus, consul in 428 B.C., who won the *spolia opima* by killing Lars Tolumnius of Veii.

CRASSUS. L. Crassus, defeated by the Parthians at Carrhae in 53 B.C.

CRAUGIS. The name of a dog; "bayer."

CREUSA. (1) The second wife of Jason, who deserted Medea to marry her. Medea revenged herself by sending Creusa a poisoned robe which destroyed her and her father Creon. (2) The wife of Aeneas, who died in the fall of Troy.

CROESUS. The last king of Lydia (560-546 B.C.), usually considered to be fabulously rich.

CUPID. The son of Venus by Mercury or by Mars or by Jupiter; a winged lad who shot arrows at anyone, causing the victim to fall in love.

CURTIUS. Manlius Curtius, a heroic knight who, in order to save his country, leaped armed and on horseback into a chasm which suddenly opened in the Forum in 360 B.C.; the chasm closed over him.

CYBELE. The mother goddess of Anatolia, worshipped with her youthful lover Attis, god of vegetation. She was the "Great Mother" whose rites were officially introduced into Rome in 204 B.C.

CYNARA. A friend or relative of Propertius.

CYNTHIA. The mistress of Propertius. Her real name was Hostia, and she was the granddaughter of a learned man identified with the Hostius who in the previous century wrote an epic on the Illyrian War. She lived in Rome in cultivated surroundings, supported by her charm and her wit, attended by at least eight slaves.

CYPRIA. The island of Cyprus, birthplace of Venus. Mt. Ida was there.

DANAE. The mother of Perseus, seduced by Jupiter in a shower of gold which penetrated the bronze tower in which her father confined her.

DANAIDS. Fifty sisters; except for one, they slew their bridegrooms and were punished in Hades.

DEIDAMIA. The mistress of Achilles on the island of Scyros; mother of Pyrrhus.

DECII. The father, son, and grandson named Publius Decius Mus, who sacrificed their lives for their country (336, 296, and 279 B.C.)

DECIUS. Same as above.

DEIANIRA. The mythological daughter of Oeneus, and wife of Hercules.

DELOS. Once a floating island in the Aegean; when Apollo and Diana were born there, it became permanently fixed in the sea.

DELPHI. A Greek city on the lower southern slopes of Parnassus, 2,000 feet above the Gulf of Corinth; famous for its shrine and oracle of Apollo.

DEMOPHOON. Son of Theseus; his beloved, Phyllis, killed herself when she was deserted by him.

DEMOSTHENES. The eminent Greek orator (385-322 B.C.).

DEUCALION. Deucalion and Pyrrha were the sole survivors of the legendary Greek great flood.

DIANA. The moon goddess; also goddess of the hunt and protectress of wild creatures; she aided women in childbirth; the Greek Artemis.

DIONYSUS. Identical with Bacchus, god of wine.

DIRCE. The second wife of Lycus, whom he preferred to Antiope. She tormented Antiope, who ultimately gained revenge with the help of her sons. (See ANTIOPE.)

DIS. Identical with Pluto. (See PLUTO.)

DNIEPER. A river 1,400 miles long in western Russia, flowing into the Black Sea (in antiquity, the Euxine Sea).

DOG STAR. The constellation Syrius; also, sometimes Procyon, a constellation which rises before the Dog Star.

DON. A river 1,100 miles long in Russia, flowing into the Sea of Azov (an arm of the Black Sea).

DOROZANTES. Alleged river in Asia Minor. (The word is dubious in the text.)

DRUID. A wise and powerful secret priest; member of a religious order in ancient Gaul, Britain, and Ireland.

DRYAD. A tree nymph.

ELECTRA. The daughter of Agamemnon who sought revenge against Clytemnestra. (See CLYTEMNESTRA.)

ELIS. A region of Greece, where Olympia is, and which therefore is associated with race horses and the Olympic games, and with Jupiter. Phidias made a chryselephantine statue of Jupiter for the great temple at Olympia.

ENDYMION. A handsome young man loved by the moon goddess (Diana) and seduced by her as he lay asleep on a mountainside; he sleeps everlastingly.

ENIPEUS. River of Thessaly. Poseidon assumed its shape when he ravished Tyro, the daughter of Salmoneus.

ENNIUS. First great Roman poet, author of the *Annals* and many other works; he lived in the second century B.C.

EPICURUS. Greek philosopher (342-270 B.C.), founder of the Epicurean school of philosophy.

EPIRUS. A region in the northwest of Greece.

ERIPHYLA. The wife of Amphiaraus; she was bribed with the gift of a golden necklace to persuade her husband to join the Seven against Thebes (see THEBAN SEVEN), even though he knew he would not return.

ERYTHIA. A mythical island in the far west, home of Geryon. (See GERYON.)

ERYTHRA. A mythical Eastern king.

ESQUILINE. One of the seven hills in Rome, a fashionable residential quarter in Propertius' day.

ETRUSCANS. Indigenous Italian people inhabiting the country between Rome and Florence, whose flourishing culture and religious and political processes influenced the Romans strongly. Most powerful in the sixth and fifth centuries B.C., they were eventually absorbed by the Romans.

EUROPA. Sister of Cadmus; she was loved by Jupiter in the form of a bull and was carried through the sea on his back from Asia Minor to Greece.

EURYPYLUS. A king of the island of Cos.

EUPHRATES. A river 1,700 miles long, flowing through ancient Persia into the Persian Gulf.

EURYTION. A Centaur slain at the wedding of Pirithous. (See PIRITHOUS.)

EVADNE. The wife of Capaneus. When he was killed by Jupiter because of blasphemy, Evadne threw herself on his funeral pyre.

EVANDER. Exiled Arcadian king who lived on the hill in Rome that was to become known as the Palatine.

FABIUS. (1) Quintus Maximus Fabius, the general in the Second Punic War who was famous for his delaying tactics, which proved effective against Hannibal. (2) One of the two colleges (Fabii) into which the Luperci, priests of Pan, were divided.

FALERNIAN. A favorite wine grown in the region of Falerii.

FIDENAE. A small town in Latium, a defense point on the Tiber just north of Rome.

FURIES. Female spirits with snaky hair, who punished the doers of unavenged crimes.

GABII. A town of Latium near Rome.

GALATEA. A sea goddess.

GALLA. Aelia Galla, a Roman lady, wife of Postumus, perhaps the sister of Aelius Gallus, prefect of Egypt.

GALLUS. A friend of Propertius; perhaps Aelius Gallus, prefect of Egypt.

GAULS. Celtic tribe from France. They invaded Rome in 368 B.C., and in 278 B.C., led by Brennus, they attacked Delphi.

GERYON. A monster dwelling in mythical Erythia, who was killed by Hercules; his cattle were taken and driven back to Greece by Hercules.

GIANTS. A mythological race of monstrous, powerful creatures; sons of Gaea (Earth) from the blood of Kronos. (See TITANS.) They tried to overcome the gods, who defeated them with the aid of Hercules.

GOLDEN FLEECE. In Greek mythology the magic fleece of a ram given by Hermes to Nephele, the wife of Athamas. When Ino, the second wife of Athamas, planned death for Nephele's children, Phrixus and Helle, the ram carried them away. Later, after arriving at Colchis, Phrixus sacrificed the ram and hung the fleece in a wood guarded by a dragon. The ram became the constellation of Aries. Phrixus married a daughter of Aetes, king of Colchis. The quest of Jason and the Argonauts was for the Golden Fleece, which Jason took after fulfilling the tasks put upon him by Aetes.

GORGON. Any of three sisters, e.g. Medusa, with snakes for hair; they were so horrible that anyone who beheld them was turned to stone.

GLAUCUS. A sea god.

HAEMON. Son of Creon, betrothed to Antigone. (See ANTIGONE.)

HAMADRYAD. A tree nymph.

HANNIBAL. The Carthaginian general who invaded Italy in the Second Punic War.

HEBE. Goddess of youth; bride of Hercules when he became a god.

HECTOR. The defender of Troy, who was killed in single combat by Achilles; son of Priam.

HELEN. Wife of Menelaus; stolen by Paris and taken to Troy; her abduction brought on the Trojan War.

HELICON. A mountain in southern Greece; the home of the Muses. The Aganippe and Hippocrene springs were there, both known for lyric inspiration.

HELLE. See GOLDEN FLEECE.

HELLEN. The eponymous founder of the Hellenes, one of the original tribes of Greeks.

HERCULES. A hero, the son of Jupiter and Alcmena, celebrated for strength and especially for achieving twelve great tasks, or "labors," imposed on him as a result of the hatred of Juno. In IV.ix Propertius describes some of the "labors" of Hercules and the legendary origin of Hercules' altar, the Ara Maxima.

HESIOD. Early Greek poet of Ascra, second in importance to Homer; the author of the *Theogony,* the *Works and Days,* and other poems; usually considered the father of pastoral and didactic poetry (ca. 800 B.C.).

HESPERIDES. Mythological gardens of the West, where the golden apples were kept. (See ATALANTA.)

HIPPODAMIA. The daughter of Oenomaus, won by Pelops, who defeated and killed her father in a chariot race.

HIPPOLYTE. The Amazonian warrior queen, bride of Theseus, and mother of Hippolytus.

HIPPOLYTUS. The son of Theseus and Hippolyte. His stepmother, Phaedra, fell in love with him but he repulsed her. Phaedra then hanged herself, accusing Hippolytus of ravishing her. Poseidon, answering the plea of Theseus, sent a sea monster which so terrified the horses of Hippolytus that they dragged him to death.

HOMER. The first and most famous Greek poet, author of the *Iliad* and the *Odyssey* (ca. ninth century B.C.).

HORATIUS. One of the brothers who fought the three brothers Curatius in a legendary contest of champions in Rome's early history.

HOROS. In IV. i a Propertius has this Babylonian astrologer advise against the poet's new intention. In the manuscripts there is no break in continuity between the two parts.

HYDRA. A nine-headed mythological serpent slain by Hercules; when any one of its heads was cut off, it was replaced by two others.

HYPERMESTRE. The one faithful bride among the fifty Danaids; she alone did not slay her husband on their wedding night. (See DANAIDS.)

ICARUS. Legendary Greek who learned from Dionysus the art of making wine. He gave wine to some Attic peasants, who became drunk and, thinking they had been poisoned, murdered Icarus. He became a star in the constellation of the Great Bear, under the name of Arcturus or Bootes.

IDA. A high mountain above Troy; there Adonis was killed by a boar.

IDAS. He and Lynceus, the sons of Aphareus, were to marry Hilaira and Phoebe, the daughters of Leucippus, but the girls were carried off by Castor and Pollux. (See also MARPESSA.)

ILIAD. Homer's great epic on the Trojan War.

ILLYRIA. A region on the eastern coast of the Adriatic sea, approximately modern Yugoslavia and Albania.

INO. See LEUCOTHOE.

IO. Beloved of Jupiter, she was turned into a cow by the jealousy of Juno and was restored to human shape only after long wanderings. In II.xxxiii she is identified with Isis. (See ISIS.)

IOPE. A slave of Cynthia.

IPHICLUS. It was his herd of cattle that Melampus intended to drive off for Neleus, so that Bias, Melampus' brother, might win the hand of Pero, the daughter of Neleus. Melampus was captured and imprisoned, but escaped and eventually succeeded in his task. In Propertius' version of the story (II.iii), Melampus himself is the suitor of Pero.

IPHIGENIA. The daughter of Agamemnon; she was sacrificed by her father at Aulis when the Greek ships were becalmed.

ISIS. The Egyptian goddess of fertility; sister and wife of Osiris.

IULUS. Son of Aeneas and grandson of Venus, identical with Ascanius.

JASON. Leader of the Argonauts in the quest for the Golden Fleece. He brought Medea back from Colchis but put her aside in favor of Creusa. (See GOLDEN FLEECE.)

JOVE. Identical with Jupiter. (See JUPITER.)

JUGURTHA. King of Numidia, captured by Marius in 104 B.C. and brought to Rome for execution.

JUNO. Queen of the gods, wife and sister of Jupiter; the Greek Hera.

JUPITER. King of the gods; the Greek Zeus.

JUPITER AMMON. Shrine of Jupiter in the Libyan desert, at the oasis of modern Siva.

JUPITER FERETRIUS. A reference to the cult of Jupiter in association with the *spolia opima* (spoils taken by the Roman commander from the enemy commander: *fero;* or from the slain enemy commander: *ferio*).

LAIS. Famous courtesan of Corinth.

LALAGE. A slave of Cynthia.

LANUVIUM. A small town southeast of Rome.

LARES. Together with the Penates, they constituted the household gods of a Roman family.

LATRIS. A slave of Cynthia.

LEDA. The wife of Tyndareus and the mother of Helen of Troy, and of the twin brothers Castor and Pollux; she was transformed into a swan by Jupiter.

LEPIDUS. One of Cornelia's sons. (See CORNELIA.)

LESBIA. A reference to Clodia, the mistress of Catullus and wife of Quintus Metellus Celer.

LESBOS. Greek island, home of the poet Sappho (ca. 600 B.C.).

LETHE. River of forgetfulness in the underworld.

LETO. Mother of Apollo and Diana; the Roman Latona.

LEUCIPPUS. Father of Hilaira and Phoebe, who were betrothed to Idas and his brother Lynceus, but were abducted by Castor and Pollux.

LEUCOTHOE. More commonly Leucothea, the name given to Ino, daughter of Cadmus and wife of Athamas, after she threw herself into the sea in a fit of madness and became a sea goddess.

LUCERES. One of the three tribes into which the Roman people divided themselves after the war with the Sabines. The other two tribes were the Ramnes, the original followers of Romulus, and the Titienses, the followers of Titus Tatius, the Sabine chief. The Luceres were the followers of Lucumo (an Etruscan word designating a leader), or of Lygmon, represented by Propertius as coming from Solonium, a town near Lanuvium.

LUPERCALIA. Libertine Roman festival in honor of Pan Lukaios (February 15).

LUPERCUS. Son of Arria. (See ARRIA.)

LYCINNA. Propertius' first love.

LYCMON. Equivalent to Lygmon, who in turn is equivalent to the Etruscan leader by name of Lucumo.

LYCORIS. The mistress of Cornelius Gallus; her real name was Cytheris.

LYCOTAS. Perhaps a pseudonym for Postumus. (See ARETHUSA.)

LYCURGUS. King of Thrace. He disapproved of the Bacchic revels and seized the god Dionysus. The god drove Lycurgus mad, so that, thinking he was chopping down a vine, the king actually slew his own son.

LYCUS. Husband of Antiope and Dirce. (See ANTIOPE.)

LYDIA. A country in western Asia Minor, the capital of which was Sardis.

LYGDAMUS. A slave of Cynthia.

LYNCEUS. A poet and friend of Propertius.

LYSIPPUS. Greek bronze sculptor of the late fourth century B.C.

MACEDONIA. A kingdom in the north of Greece; birthplace of Philip, the father of Alexander the Great.

MAECENAS. Wealthy Roman knight (ca. 70-8 B.C.); patron of Propertius, Vergil, and Horace, and close friend of Augustus.

MAENAD. A nymph in attendance upon Bacchus or a female initiate (Bacchante) in the Bacchic rites.

MAMURIUS. Mamurius Venturius, a mythical worker in bronze in the reign of Numa.

MARCELLUS. (1) The Roman general Marcus Claudius Marcellus (ca.

268-208 B.C.). (2) The young Marcellus, nephew of Augustus and son of Octavia, who died at the age of twenty in 23 B.C. and is eulogized in III.xviii and in *Aeneid* VI. 882-886.

MARCIA. The *aqua Marcia* was the water supplied by the aqueduct built by Quintus Marcius Rex in 144 B.C. The water was famous for its purity.

MARIUS. Gaius Marius, the famous Roman general who defeated the Teutons and Cimbri in 102 and 101 B.C.

MARO. A companion of Bacchus, god of wine.

MARPESSA. Wife of Idas, whom she chose in preference to Apollo.

MARS. God of war; the Greek Ares.

MAUSOLUS. King of Caria (died in 353 B.C.), whose wife Artemisia erected a great tomb in his memory, called the Mausoleum.

MEANDER. A winding river in Asia Minor.

MEDEA. The Colchian princess whom Jason took home with him when he returned from the quest for the Golden Fleece. When Jason deserted her in favor of Creusa, Medea poisoned both Creusa and her father, and killed her own sons by Jason. (See GOLDEN FLEECE.)

MEDIANS. Inhabitants of a country in the Middle East, now northwestern Iran.

MELAMPUS. According to Propertius (II.iii), he was the suitor of Pero, rather than, as in the usual story, the man who tried to help his brother win the girl. (See IPHICLUS.)

MELEAGER. Son of Althea. He killed the Calydonian boar and Althea's brothers as well; so she caused the death of her son by burning a log that she had removed from the fire at his birth, when it was foretold that he would die when the log was consumed.

MEMNON. Son of the goddess of the dawn (Aurora) and king of Ethiopia. He came to aid the Trojans and was slain by Achilles in the Trojan War.

MENANDER. Greek poet and dramatist, best-known writer of New Comedy (ca. 343-291 B.C.).

MEMPHIS. A city in Egypt near the mouth of the Nile river.

MENELAUS. King of Sparta, brother of Agamemnon, and husband of Helen. The abduction of Helen by Paris brought Menelaus and the Greeks to wage the Trojan War.

MENTOR. Famous Greek silversmith.

MERCURY. Messenger of the gods; the Greek Hermes.

MEVANIA. An Italian town near Assisi; modern Bevagna.

MILANION. The successful suitor of Atalanta. (See ATALANTA.)

MINERVA. Goddess of wisdom; the Greek Athena.

MINOS. King of Knossus in Crete; after his death, he became a judge of the dead. (See SCYLLA.)

MINOTAUR. A monster with the body of a man and the head of a bull (in some versions with the body of a bull and the head of a man), confined by Minos in the Labyrinth in Crete which was built by Daedalus. Annually he was fed seven youths and seven maidens from Athens, until he was killed by Theseus.

MUSE. Any of the nine goddesses who presided over literature and the arts and sciences.

MUTINA. A besieged town which Octavian relieved by a victory over Antony in 43 B.C.; modern Modena.

MYCENAE. An ancient Greek city in the northeastern Peloponnesus.

MYRON. Athenian sculptor (ca. 430 B.C.).

MYRRHA. Mother of Adonis by her own father Cinyras, for whom she entertained an unnatural passion, in consequence of which she was changed into a myrtle tree.

MYS. Greek silversmith.

MYSIA. Kingdom in Asia Minor ruled by Telephus.

NAIS. A naiad, that is, water nymph.

NAUPLIUS. By luring the homecoming Greek ships to destruction on the promontory of Caphareus, Nauplius was revenged for the death of his son Palamedes in the Trojan War. Palamedes had been wrongly adjudged a traitor and stoned to death by the Greeks.

NAXOS. Greek island on which Ariadne was abandoned. (See ARIADNE.)

NEMI. Volcanic lake and forested region sacred to Diana in the Alban hills near Rome.

NEREIDS. Sea nymphs.

NEREUS. Sea god; father of the Nereids.

NESTOR. Oldest Greek warrior in the Trojan War.

NIOBE. She boasted that her six sons and six daughters were more beautiful than Apollo and Diana. Diana punished her by slaying her children and turning Niobe into stone.

NISUS. See SCYLLA.

NOMAS. A slave of Cynthia.

NOMENTUM. A small town four miles north of Rome.

NYSA. A legendary mountain or town where Bacchus was brought up by the nymphs.

OCNUS. An industrious man whose hard-earned income was steadily consumed by his wife's extravagance. In Polygnotus' famous painting of the underworld, Ocnus was represented as being punished for his folly by having to twist a rope of straw, which an ass devoured continually at the other end. "To twist the rope of Ocnus" became a proverbial expression.

ODYSSEUS. Identical with Ulysses; hero of Homer's *Odyssey,* which celebrates his voyage home from the Trojan War.

OEDIPUS. Ruler of Thebes. Unknowingly, he killed his father and married his mother.

OENONE. A nymph of Mount Ida, loved by Paris, who then deserted her.

OETA. Mountain; scene of Hercules' death and transfiguration, as well as his love for Hebe. (See HEBE.)

OLYMPUS. A mountain of nearly 9,600 feet on the borders of Macedonia and Thessaly; regarded as the home of the gods.

OMPHALE. A queen of Lydia whom Hercules loved and served in the guise of a woman.

ORESTES. Son of Agamemnon and Clytemnestra; he killed his mother to revenge her killing of his father. His story is told by both Aeschylus and Euripides.

ORION. A gigantic hunter, referred to (as early as Homer) as identical with the constellation. He loved Eos and was killed by Diana. In another legend he loved Merope, was blinded by her father, and waded through the sea until he came to the farthest eastern point and there got back his sight from the sun's rays.

ORITHYIA. Daughter of Erechtheus, king of Athens. She was long sued for by Boreas (the North Wind), who finally became tired of being put off by her father and abducted her to Thrace, where she became the mother of Zetes and Calais.

OROPS. Babylonian astrologer.

ORPHEUS. Legendary Thracian hero, founder of music and agriculture.

OSSA. Mountain in Thessaly. Two giants, Otus and Ephialtes, tried to pile Mount Pelion atop Mount Ossa and so storm the heights of heaven.

PAESTUM. A coastal town in southern Italy famous for its roses.

PAETUS. A friend of Propertius, drowned at sea.

PAGASA. The port in Greece from which the Argo set out on the quest for the Golden Fleece. (See GOLDEN FLEECE.)

PALATINE. One of the seven hills in Rome, where the emperor resided.

PALES. Italian goddess of shepherds. Straw-burning was a purification rite in her honor.

PALLAS. Athena, Greek goddess of wisdom; the Roman Minerva.

PANTHUS. One of Cynthia's lovers.

PARILIA. The Roman feast of Pales, goddess of flocks, which took place on April 21, the day of the foundation of Rome. (See PALES.)

PARIS. Trojan prince, son of Priam, who loved Helen and took her away from Sparta to Troy, in spite of the fact that she was already married to Menelaus; he thus provoked the Trojan War.

PARNASSUS. Outlying spur of the Pindus range of mountains, rising to a height of 8,200 feet. On Parnassus were Delphi and the Castalian Spring. The mountain was considered sacred to Apollo and the Muses.

PARRHASIUS. A Greek painter (ca. 400 B.C.), famous for his detailed work.

PARTHENIE. Cynthia's nurse.

PARTHIA. Ancient country, northeast Persia. The expedition against the Parthians, often anticipated in the verses of Augustan poets, never took place. By negotiations in 20 B.C. the standards and spoils taken from Crassus in the defeat at Carrhae (53 B.C.) were returned to Rome.

PASIPHAE. Wife of Minos; she fell in love with a bull, and became the mother of the Minotaur. (See MINOTAUR.)

PATROCLUS. Friend of Achilles in the Trojan War; killed by Hector, who in turn was killed by Achilles in revenge.

PAULLUS. L. Aemilius Paullus Lepidus, whose wife Cornelia's "funeral oration" was composed by Propertius in IV.xi.

PEGASUS. Magical winged horse, tamed by Bellerophon. He is said to have struck the ground of Mount Helicon with his hoof, causing the spring of Hippocrene to gush forth.

PELEUS. The father of Achilles.

PELION. Mountain in Thessaly. (See OSSA.)

PELUSIUM. A fortress on a branch of the Nile river, captured by Augustus.

PENELOPE. The faithful wife of Ulysses, who waited for him to come home from the Trojan War.

PENTHESILEA. Amazonian queen, a combatant in the Trojan War on the side of the Trojans. She was slain by Achilles, who is said to have fallen in love with her when her helmet was removed and he saw the beauty of her dead face.

PENTHEUS. King of Thebes and son of Agave. Agave dismembered her son when he was caught witnessing the Bacchic rites.

PERILLUS. Craftsman who designed a bronze bull as an instrument of torture, for roasting people. When he presented the bull to Phalaris, the tyrant of Agrigentum, Phalaris ordered Perillus to be the first victim.

PERO. Daughter of Neleus, and beloved of Bias, or of Melampus. (See IPHICLUS.)

PERSEPHONE. Daughter of Demeter (Mother Earth) and goddess-queen of the underworld. She spends two-thirds of the year with her mother (symbolizing the return of life to the earth) and one-third of the year as the goddess of death beneath the earth.

PERSEUS. (1) Mythological figure; son of Danae. He cut off Medusa's head. (2) Historical figure; king of Macedonia, who was defeated by Aemilius Paullus, Cornelia's ancestor, at Pydna in 168 B.C. He claimed to be descended both from Achilles and Hercules.

PERUGIA. The scene of a battle in 41 B.C., in which Octavian defeated L. Antonius (youngest brother of Marc Antony). Perusia (modern Perugia) was an Etruscan town near the Umbrian town of Assisi which Propertius mentions (IV.i) as his home.

PETALE. A slave of Cynthia.

PHAEDRA. Sister of Ariadne and Pasiphae, and wife of Theseus. She committed suicide over the revelation of her love for Hippolytus. (See HIPPOLYTUS.)

PHAROS. An island with a lighthouse, in the harbor at Alexandria.

PHASIS. A river of Colchis on the Black Sea.

PHIDIAS. The most famous Greek sculptor (ca. 490-430 B.C.).

PHILETAS. An Alexandrian poet from the island of Cos; like Callimachus, he was a strong influence upon Propertius.

PHILIPPI. A town in Macedonia. In 42 B.C. it was the scene of the double battle in which Antony defeated M. Brutus and Cassius.

PHILOCTETES. He was left at Lemnos on the way to Troy because of an infected wound, which was healed by Machaon when Philoctetes was forcibly returned to the Greek army.

PHILOMELA. The sister of Procne, lured away from her father Pandion and raped by Terues, the husband of Procne, who then cut out her tongue. She and Procne eventually secured revenge against Tereus by serving him his son Itys at a meal. Tereus pursued the women but he was turned into a hoopoe, Procne into a nightingale, and Philomela into a swallow. A later tradition reverses the transformation of the two women and makes Philomela the nightingale and Procne the swallow.

PHINEUS. Blind seer and king of Bithynia; plagued by the Harpies (half birds, half maidens, and spirits of mischief), who defiled or stole all his food.

PHLEGREAN FIELDS. The volcanic region north of Naples, considered the scene of the legendary battle between the gods and giants. (See GIANTS.)

PHOEBUS. Identical with Apollo. (See APOLLO.)

PHOENICIA. A trading colony on the coast of Asia Minor; its main cities were Byblus, Tyre, and Sidon.

PHOENIX. Achilles' tutor, blinded by his father but healed by Chiron. He accompanied Achilles to Troy.

PHRYGIA. The general region of Asia Minor where Troy was located.

PHRYNE. A courtesan of Athens.

PHYLLIS. Beloved of Demophoon; she killed herself when deserted by him.

PINDAR. Greek lyric poet (518-438 B.C.).

PINDUS. A mountain on the borders of Macedonia and Epirus.

PIRITHOUS. Friend of Theseus; his bride Ischomache was abducted by the Centaurs at their wedding banquet.

PLEIADES. Daughters of Atlas, and virgin companions of Diana, who were transformed into doves to escape the advances of Orion, and then were themselves placed among the stars.

PLUTO. King of the underworld; the Greek Dis.

POLLUX. Twin brother of Castor. (See CASTOR.)

POLYMESTOR. King of Thrace and guardian of Polydorus, the son whom Priam placed in Polymestor's care during the Trojan War. Polymestor murdered Polydorus for the sake of his gold.

POLYPHEMUS. Son of Neptune; the one-eyed Cyclops blinded by Ulysses; lover of the nymph Galatea.

POMPEY. Gnaeus Pompeius Magnus (106-48 B.C.), the Roman general defeated by Caesar at Pharsalus in 48 B.C. at the close of the Civil War. In flight to Egypt, Pompey was stabbed to death as he landed. "The colonnade of Pompey," referred to in II.xxxii, was built in 53 B.C. and stood near Pompey's theatre on the Campus Martius. "Parading the streets to be admired" (IV.viii) contains a reference to the sheltered walk provided by the "shade of Pompey" in this colonnade.

PONTICUS. A friend of Propertius and an epic poet.

POSTUMUS. A friend of Propertius; the husband of Aelia Galla, and perhaps identified with Lycotas. (See ARETHUSA.)

PRAENESTE. Hill town twenty miles east of Rome, famous for its oracle of Fortuna Primigenia; modern Palestrina.

PRAXITELES. Famous Greek sculptor; an Athenian of the middle of the fourth century B.C.

PRIAM. Aged king of Troy in the Trojan War.

PROMETHEUS. Son of the Titan Iapetus. He defied Zeus by bringing fire to man. (See TITANS.)

PROTEUS. An oracular sea god who could assume different shapes. If caught and held through his many shapes, he was compelled to answer questions.

PTOLEMY. The name of all the Macedonian kings of Egypt. Ptolemy XIII was the brother of Cleopatra VII; he was born in 63 and died in 47 B.C. "Ptolemy's Pharos on the conquered shore" (II.i) refers to the famous lighthouse on the island of Pharos at the entrance to the harbor of Alexandria.

PYRRHUS. King of Epirus, who invaded Italy in the early years of the third century B.C. and was defeated by Rome with great difficulty.

QUINTILIA. The mistress of Propertius' friend, the poet Calvus.

RAMNES. Tribe named after the followers of Romulus. (See LUCERES.).

REMUS. Twin brother of Romulus. His name is used interchangeably with that of Romulus, for metrical reasons.

RHADAMANTHUS. Brother of Minos and a judge of the dead.

ROMULUS. Legendary founder of Rome.

SABINE RAPE. The Sabine women were allegedly raped to supply wives for the womenless followers of Romulus.

SABINES. Indigenous Italians dwelling northeast of Rome, who fought the early Romans but by 449 B.C. had been overcome and taken into the Roman orbit.

SACRED WAY. *Via Sacra,* first street of ancient Rome to be established on the low ground beneath the hills. According to tradition, on this road Romulus made his treaty with the Sabine chief Tatius.

SATURN. Father of Jupiter; king of the gods during the "Golden Age;" a fertility god of the Italians.

SCAEAN GATE. A gate of Troy before which Achilles was slain.

SCAMANDER. A river on the plain of Troy.

SCIPIO. A distinguished Roman family whose members figured largely in the conquest of Carthage during the three Punic Wars (264-241; 218-201; 149-146 B.C.).

SCRIBONIA. Mother of Cornelia; afterward the wife of Augustus.

SCYLLA. (1) Monster dwelling in a cave on the Italian shore of the Straits of Messina; usually paired with Charybdis. (See CHARYBDIS.) (2) Daughter of Nisus, king of Megara. Nisus had a golden or purple lock of hair, and as long as it remained uncut, so long was his life to last. For love of Minos, king of Crete, Scylla cut Nisus' lock of hair. Nisus died and Megara was taken.

SCYTHIA. The name given by the Greeks to the country between the Carpathians and the river Don.

SEMELE. Mother of Bacchus by Jupiter. When she asked Jupiter to come to her in his full power, Semele was killed by the thunderbolt; but Jupiter saved the life of Bacchus by cutting open his own thigh and concealing the child there until the period of gestation was completed.

SEMIRAMIS. Sammuramat, Persian queen who founded Babylon; wife of the Assyrian king Shamski-Adad V; regent (810-805 B.C.) during the minority of her son Adad-Nirari III.

SIBYL. Ecstatic aged priestess of Apollo; particularly the Cumaean Sibyl, whose shrine was a cave near lake Avernus just north of Naples.

SILENUS. Like Satyrs, the Sileni are "spirits of wild life in woods and hills," with features of animal nature, either of a horse or a goat. The most famous Silenus was an ugly old man who was wise, sensual, and poetic.

SIMOIS. A river of Troy.

SINIS. A robber who killed his victims by bending two pine trees together and tying them between the trees. When the trees swung apart, the victims were torn in two. Sinis was put to death by Theseus.

SIRENS. Half-women, half-birds, endowed with a capacity for spellbinding song. They lured sailors to their death on their island. Ulysses was the first to escape them; he tied himself to the mast and stopped the ears of his sailors with wax.

SISYPHUS. King of Corinth, who was condemned for his sins to roll a rock uphill for all eternity. The moment the rock reached the top, it rolled down again.

SOCRATES. The famous Athenian philosopher (469-399 B.C.), whose teachings were recorded for history by Plato.

SPARTA. Important city in the Peloponnesus; Sparta conquered Athens in the Peloponnesian War (431-404 B.C.).

STYX. A river of Arcadia, the water of which was thought poisonous; considered one of the nine rivers of the underworld.

SUBURA. A quarter of Rome lying between the Esquiline, Viminal, and Quirinal; a great haunt of courtesans.

SYCAMBRI. The Sycambri defeated the Romans under Marcus Lollius in Gaul in 16 B.C.; Augustus then went to Gaul to deal with the situation.

SYMPLEGADES. The clashing rocks between which the Argo sailed successfully. (See ARGO.)

SYPHAX. Libyan king. He deserted Rome and allied himself with Carthage in the second Punic War; he was defeated by Scipio and brought a captive to Rome in 201 B.C.

SYRTES. A treacherous offshore gulf on the coast of North Africa.

TANTALUS. An immortal who stole the food of the gods and gave it to mortals. His everlasting punishment is to be hungry and thirsty, standing in water up to his chin, with fruit-laden trees over his head. When he tries to drink, the water disappears; if he reaches for the fruit, the wind blows it away. Tantalus was the ancestor of the Pelops line which continued on to Atreus and Agamemnon, and he was the father of Niobe.

TARPEIA. (1) In I.xvi and III.xi the reference is to one of the original Vestals appointed by Numa. The name signifies the ancient sanctity of the region on the Capitoline hill, the *mons Tarpeius*. (2) In IV.iv the reference is to Tarpeia who betrayed the citadel of Rome to Tatius; she was killed for her disloyalty. Propertius changes the legend by making Tarpeia's passion for the Sabine king Tatius her main motive in betraying the citadel.

TATIUS. Titus Tatius, king of the Sabines, who defeated Romulus and became joint king of Rome.

TELEPHUS. King of Mysia; he was wounded by Achilles' spear and then healed by rust from the same spear.

THAIS. Athenian courtesan who accompanied Alexander the Great on his expedition to Asia; characterized in a play by Menander.

THEBAN SEVEN. The Seven against Thebes: the seven champions who tried to wrest Thebes from the power of Eteocles (son of Oedipus). They were Adrastus, Capaneus, Hippomedon, Amphiaraus, Parthenopaeus, Tydeus, and Polynices (another son of Oedipus). All of the assailants fell, except Adrastus; and both brothers met their death, as had been prophesied.

THEBES. Famous Greek city founded by Cadmus; later under the rule of Oedipus, and fought over by his two sons, Eteocles and Polynices. (See THEBAN SEVEN.)

THEIODAMAS. Father of Hylas. Hylas accompanied Hercules on the voyage of the Argonauts. When he paused to draw water from a fountain, the nymphs of the fountain drew the handsome lad down into the water. Thereafter the Mysians of the region sacrificed to Hylas annually at the fountain.

THETIS. Sea nymph, and mother of Achilles. She bathed her son in the river Styx, rendering him invulnerable except for a place on his heel.

THESEUS. Famous Greek hero, conqueror of the Minotaur, and ruler of Athens.

TIBER. Italian river which flows through Rome.

TIRESIAS. Blind seer of Thebes; he plays an important part in the story of Oedipus and the wars against Thebes. (See THEBAN SEVEN.)

TITANS. The older gods who preceded the Olympians: Oceanus, Coeus, Crius, Hyperion, Iapetos, Theia, Rhea, Themis, Mnemosyne, Phoebe, Tethys, and Kronos. Under Kronos they fought against Jupiter but were overcome by him, and the Olympians became the supreme gods.

TITHONUS. Consort of the goddess of the dawn (Aurora); his immortality was not accompanied by eternal youth.

TITIENSES. See LUCERES.

TITYUS. A giant who offered violence to Leto and was killed by Apollo and Diana. He was condemned to be devoured eternally by a vulture in Hades.

TITYRUS. A shepherd mentioned in Vergil's *Eclogues.*

TIVOLI. A town on the Anio in the Sabine hills; modern Tivoli.

TOLUMNIUS. King of Veii, who was killed by Romulus in combat.

TRITON. A sea god, merman, and hornblower of the deep.

TRIVIA. Diana "of the Crossways," one of the aspects of the moon goddess.

TROJAN WAR. When Paris, son of Priam of Troy, abducted Helen, wife of Menelaus of Sparta, the Greeks laid siege to the city and eventually conquered it. The war is celebrated in Homer's *Iliad.* The survivors of Troy followed Aeneas to Italy; the story is told in the *Aeneid* of Vergil.

TROY. Priam's ancient capital in Phrygia, conquered by Greeks in the Trojan War.

TULLUS. A friend of Propertius.

TUSCANY. A region of west central Italy.

TUSCULUM. A small town in the Alban hills near Rome.

TYNDAREUS. King of Sparta; husband of Leda; father of Helen, Clytemnestra, and the twins Castor and Pollux.

TYRE. A city of Phoenicia, famous for its purple dye.

TYRO. Daughter of Salmoneus; she was ravished by Neptune in the guise of the river god Enipeus.

ULYSSES. Identical with Odysseus. (See ODYSSEUS.)

UMBRIA. An important Etruscan region in central Italy.

VARRO. A poet of the Alexandrian school, born at Atax. He translated the *Argonautica* of Apollonius Rhodius, and subsequently wrote elegies in honor of his mistress Leucadia.

VEII. An ancient town of Etruria, north of Rome.

VENUS. Roman goddess of love, alleged mother of Aeneas and ancestress of the Julian family.

VERGIL. Famous Latin poet (70-19 B.C.), author of the *Aeneid,* the *Georgics,* and the *Eclogues.*

VERTUMNUS. Roman god of the seasons ("Changeable"), associated with the seasons and the fruits of the earth. His image stood in Rome's Vicus Tuscus which leads from the Velabrum to the Forum Romanorum.

VESTA. Roman goddess of the household and hearth; also of flocks and herds.

VESTALS. Virgin priestesses of Vesta, whose house was in the Forum Romanorum.

VIRDOMARUS. King of the Insubres; he was slain by M. Claudius Marcellus at Clastidium in 222 B.C.

XERXES. Persian king (486-465 B.C.); he attempted to cut a canal across the promontory of Mount Athos.

ZETES. A winged son of the North Wind (Boreas).

ZETHUS. Brother of Amphion, and son of Antiope and Jupiter. (See ANTIOPE.)